Bill's
Italian
Food

Bill Granger

Bill's
Italian
Food

Bill Granger

PHOTOGRAPHY BY MIKKEL VANG

HarperCollins*Publishers*

CONTENTS

ITALIA.

'These people really know how to live,' I decide every time I visit Italy. Italians look as if they're thoroughly enjoying life as stylish extras on the set of *Roman Holiday*. They don't suck coffee from disposable sippy-cups on the bus; they lean against marble bars and drink tiny grown-up espressos. They don't dash down takeaway burgers over computer keyboards; they unwrap paper parcels of spiced salami or creamy cheese in shaded parks. And, while much of the world hums with anxiety in rush-hour traffic, the Italians dress up for the daily

passeggiata before zipping off on
a shiny red Vespa to eat gelato with
a glossy-haired Audrey Hepburn ...
My imagination has run away with
me, but Italians do seem to have
made some great lifestyle choices
– just don't mention politics, please!
Sitting down to eat well with family
and friends takes high priority,
yet no stress accompanies that
expectation and there's a refreshing
lack of artifice about what is put on
the table. This country is the home
of the slow cooking movement, yet
no Italian would waste time faffing
around with already-perfect fresh
ingredients (how they must sigh
at our foams and deconstructions).
The regional dishes are as old as
the hills they come from, yet the
freshness of the ingredients gives
them modernity. Rich and poor,
all are able to eat well in Italy. It's
this joy of life and respect for food
that I resolve to take home with
me every time I visit. Yes, the
Italians really know how to live.

If you need to cheat (and, goodness knows, there are plenty of times when that way sanity lies) you can buy all these bits and pieces at a deli or supermarket. But, if there's ever a lovely slow empty afternoon when you're in the mood for pottering in the kitchen and stocking the fridge, here are some ideas to work with. They'll give you the basic foundations for many Italian dishes and take the pressure off during the week. None of these are complicated, but all will lift any meal from basic to *bellissimo*. Home-made focaccia can make a meal out of anything – in the best possible way. And, while pasta with supermarket pesto isn't a dish that generates much excitement, home-made pesto certainly does.

Cucina

PANTRY

SOFFRITTO IN OLIVE OIL

Garlic, onion and celery make up the 'holy trinity' of much Mediterranean cooking and a finely diced soffritto is the base for just about any soup, stew, sauce or braise created on an Italian stove. I'm a bit of a rebel here: I tend to chop my ingredients a little less finely than the average Italian cook.

4 tablespoons olive oil, plus extra for storing
5 carrots, sliced
4 onions, sliced
5 celery sticks, sliced
6 garlic cloves, sliced

Heat the olive oil in a large deep-sided saucepan. Add the carrot, onion and celery and season generously with sea salt. Cook, stirring frequently, for 25–30 minutes, or until the vegetables soften and turn a light golden colour.

Add the garlic and continue to cook for 5 minutes. Remove from the heat and allow to cool to room temperature. Spoon into sterilised jars and cover with a layer of olive oil. Alternatively, pack the soffritto into small plastic containers and freeze until ready to use. MAKES 1KG

Making soffritto in advance is a time-saving revelation. This finely chopped flavour base can be kept under a thin layer of olive oil in a jar in the fridge, or even frozen (without the oil). So if, like me, you're often left with a couple of slightly less-than-crunchy celery stalks or carrots in the vegetable crisper, quickly dice, cook and keep.

ROASTED TOMATO PASSATA

Roasting is the best way to haul flavour from not–so–perfect tomatoes and give them some punch.

1kg ripe tomatoes, roughly chopped
2 garlic cloves, sliced
2 tablespoons thyme leaves
½ teaspoon crushed chilli
½ teaspoon caster sugar
2 tablespoons olive oil

Preheat the oven to 200°C/gas mark 6. Spread the tomato on a baking tray, sprinkle over the garlic, thyme, chilli and sugar, and season with sea salt. Drizzle with oil and roast for 45 minutes. Remove from the oven and tip into the bowl of a food processor. Whiz to a purée.

The passata can be used immediately, or kept chilled for up to 3 days and reheated before using.
MAKES 750ML

NO-COOK TOMATO SAUCE

This sauce is perfect when you have decided to grow tomatoes and are feeling rather smug about your new-found green thumb (sorry to shatter your illusions, but even I can grow tomatoes). Stir it into pasta, perhaps with torn mozzarella or capers, spread on toasted crusty bread or spoon into bottling jars for friends.

½ teaspoon fennel seeds
1kg very ripe tomatoes
2 garlic cloves
4 tablespoons olive oil

Toast the fennel seeds in a frying pan over low heat, shaking the pan occasionally, until the fennel releases its aroma. Tip into a mortar and pestle and coarsely grind. Set aside.

Whiz all the ingredients together in a food processor or, if making the sauce by hand, grate the tomatoes into a bowl then crush in the garlic and stir in the olive oil and ground fennel. Season with sea salt and set aside for 30 minutes to allow the flavours to mingle. **MAKES 1 LITRE**

BASIC FOCACCIA DOUGH

7g sachet instant yeast
500g strong white bread flour
115g strong wholemeal bread flour
1 teaspoon salt
1 tablespoon sugar
3 tablespoons olive oil, plus extra for greasing

Combine all the dry ingredients in a bowl and make
a well in the centre. Mix the oil and 300ml tepid
water in a jug and pour into the well, stirring until
the dough is soft. If the dough is too dry add a little
more liquid; if too wet, a little more flour.

Turn onto a lightly floured surface and knead for
10 minutes, until elastic. Place in a lightly oiled
bowl, cover with oiled cling film and leave to rise
in a warm place for 45 minutes–1 hour.

Tip the risen dough onto the floured surface and
knock back to its original size by punching it gently.
Place on a lightly oiled baking sheet and stretch
out to a square roughly 28cm x 28cm. Cover with
lightly oiled cling film and leave to rise for another
30 minutes. MAKES DOUGH FOR 1 LOAF

Years ago an Italian girl invited us over for lunch: just rotisserie chicken, salad and store-bought pesto. Then she opened the oven and lifted out a freshly baked focaccia. Sprinkled with olive oil and sea salt, that bread turned a simple meal into one I haven't forgotten.

ONION, ARTICHOKE AND BLACK OLIVE FOCACCIA

basic focaccia dough (see page 22)
1 red onion, cut into wedges
6 artichokes in olive oil,
  drained and halved
handful pitted black olives
olive oil, for drizzling

Preheat the oven to 220°C/gas mark 7. Make dimples in the dough with your fingertips. Gently push the topping ingredients into the dimples, then drizzle with olive oil and season with sea salt. Bake for 25–30 minutes, until golden and cooked through. Serve warm. **MAKES 1 LOAF**

ROSEMARY AND POTATO FOCACCIA

basic focaccia dough (see page 22)
knob of butter
1 tablespoon olive oil, plus extra for drizzling
315g small new potatoes, halved
3 rosemary sprigs, leaves picked

Start making the topping once the dough has been shaped and set aside for its second rise.

Preheat the oven to 220°C/gas mark 7. Heat the butter and olive oil in a large non-stick frying pan. Tip in the potatoes and rosemary, and cook for 15–20 minutes, turning occasionally, until the potatoes are just tender and lightly golden. Remove from the heat and allow to cool slightly.

Make dimples in the dough with your fingertips. Top with the potato and rosemary mix, pushing the topping into the dimples. Drizzle with olive oil and sprinkle over a little sea salt. Bake for 25–30 minutes, until golden and cooked through. Serve warm. **MAKES 1 LOAF**

VEGETABLE BREAD ROLLS

basic focaccia dough (see page 22)
6 slices grilled aubergine in olive oil,
    drained and halved lengthways
6 roasted red peppers in olive oil,
    drained and halved lengthways
3 rosemary sprigs, broken up
olive oil, for greasing and drizzling

Make the dough by following the instructions in the
basic recipe but only leave it to rise for 30 minutes.

Divide the dough into 12 balls and roll each into
6cm x 12cm rectangles. Lay a slice of aubergine
and red pepper over each one, add some rosemary
and season with sea salt and freshly ground black
pepper. Roll up into scrolls and transfer to an oiled
baking tray. Cover with oiled cling film and leave
to rise for 15 minutes.

Preheat the oven to 220°C/gas mark 7. Drizzle the
scrolls with olive oil and bake for 25–30 minutes,
until golden and cooked through. MAKES 12 ROLLS

These are inspired by my daughters Inès and Bunny, who sneak away with tiny handfuls of dough when I'm cooking any sort of bread. Later, on the edge of my baking tray, I discover lovely little twisted rolls stuffed with morsels of vegetables, herbs or cheese. Serve with soup or an antipasto platter.

EASY RAVIOLI

400g '00' flour
4 eggs, lightly beaten, plus 2 eggs for glazing
1 teaspoon olive oil
1 quantity ravioli filling (see recipes)
semolina, for dusting
60g butter, to serve
freshly grated parmesan cheese or
    a squeeze of lemon juice, to serve

Put the flour into the bowl of a food processor, add the beaten eggs and olive oil and pulse until the mixture resembles large grains of couscous. Remove from the processor and bring the mixture together with your hands. Tip out onto a lightly floured work surface and knead for 10 minutes, until the dough is very smooth and elastic. Wrap in cling film and allow to rest for 30 minutes.

Divide the dough into 4 pieces and pass through all the stages on your pasta machine. You should end up with 4 long, thin sheets of pasta. Divide each sheet in half and lay them on a surface dusted with semolina.

Cut the pasta sheets into large triangles or rectangles and add 1 tablespoon of filling to one end of each piece. Lightly brush the edge of the pasta with beaten egg and fold the dough over to completely encase the filling. Press down with your fingers to seal, making sure you push out any air as you go. Transfer to a tray generously dusted with semolina and set aside for about 15 minutes to allow the ravioli to dry out.

Bring a large pan of salted water to the boil. Drop in the ravioli and cook for 3–4 minutes. Remove with a slotted spoon and serve with melted butter and lots of freshly ground black pepper. If you've made one of the vegetarian ravioli, add grated parmesan to serve. For the prawn ravioli, finish with a light squeeze of lemon juice. SERVES 4–6

PRAWN AND DILL RAVIOLI FILLING

375g raw peeled prawns
2 tablespoons double cream
juice ½ lemon
2 tablespoons roughly chopped dill

Whiz half the prawns in a food processor with the cream, until smooth. Finely chop the remaining prawns and mix with the blended prawns, lemon juice and the dill. Season with sea salt and freshly ground black pepper, then use to fill the ravioli.

RICOTTA, LEMON AND MINT RAVIOLI FILLING

250g ricotta cheese
100g parmesan cheese, freshly grated
grated zest 1 lemon
large handful mint leaves, roughly chopped

Mix all the ingredients together with some sea salt and freshly ground black pepper, then use to fill the ravioli.

POTATO, PECORINO AND BASIL RAVIOLI FILLING

1 x 400g baking potato
½ garlic clove, crushed
3 tablespoons freshly grated pecorino cheese
small bunch basil, leaves chopped

Preheat the oven to 200°C/gas mark 6. Bake the whole potato for 1 hour, or until tender and cooked through. Carefully cut open and scoop the flesh into a bowl with the garlic, pecorino and basil. Mash together and add some sea salt and freshly ground black pepper. Set aside to cool before using to fill the ravioli.

SALSA VERDE

1 tablespoon capers, drained and chopped
2 anchovy fillets, chopped
1 garlic clove, finely chopped
small bunch flat-leaf parsley, finely chopped
small bunch chervil, finely chopped
grated zest ½ lemon
3 tablespoons olive oil, plus extra if storing
½ teaspoon red wine vinegar

Stir all the ingredients together in a bowl and
season with sea salt and freshly ground black
pepper. Set aside for 1 hour to allow the flavours
to develop.

If not using straight away, spoon into a container,
pour in enough olive oil to cover by 0.5cm and seal
with a tight-fitting lid. Keep in the fridge for up to
1 week. SERVES 4–6

Pesto is a favourite recipe,
for the simplest but most
satisfying of reasons: what
child doesn't eat pasta pesto?
For some reason it seems to
break through the 'no green'
rule. So, stir these through
pasta for the bambini, or serve
for grown-ups with hot grilled
meat or cold leftover roasts.
Salsa verde is great with fish,
and roasted pepper and almond
pesto was put on this earth to
be eaten with sausages.

PARSLEY AND WALNUT PESTO

50g roasted walnuts, roughly chopped
2 garlic cloves, roughly chopped
4 tablespoons freshly grated parmesan cheese
large bunch flat-leaf parsley, roughly chopped
4 tablespoons olive oil, plus extra if storing

Mix together the walnuts, garlic, parmesan and parsley in a bowl, until well combined. Add some sea salt and freshly ground black pepper then stir in the olive oil.

If not using straight away, spoon into a container, pour in enough olive oil to cover by 0.5cm and seal with a tight-fitting lid. Keep in the fridge for up to 1 week. SERVES 4–6

PISTACHIO AND CHILLI PESTO

50g roasted pistachios, roughly chopped
2 garlic cloves, roughly chopped
small bunch mint, roughly chopped
small bunch flat-leaf parsley, roughly chopped
50g parmesan cheese, freshly grated
1 red chilli, finely chopped
4 tablespoons olive oil, plus extra if storing

Mix together the pistachios, garlic, herbs, parmesan and chilli in a bowl, until well combined. Add some sea salt and stir in the olive oil.

If not using straight away, spoon into a container, pour in enough olive oil to cover by 0.5cm and seal with a tight-fitting lid. Keep in the fridge for up to 1 week. SERVES 4–6

ROASTED PEPPER AND ALMOND PESTO

4 roasted red peppers in olive oil,
    drained and roughly chopped
2 garlic cloves, roughly chopped
½ teaspoon dried chilli flakes
50g roasted almonds, roughly chopped
4 tablespoons freshly grated parmesan cheese
125ml olive oil, plus extra if storing

Put the red peppers, garlic, chilli flakes and almonds into the bowl of a food processor. Whiz to a rough paste then stir in the parmesan, olive oil and some sea salt.

If not using straight away, spoon into a container, pour in enough olive oil to cover by 0.5cm and seal with a tight-fitting lid. Keep in the fridge for up to 1 week. SERVES 4–6

BASIC PIZZA DOUGH

2 teaspoons dried instant yeast
1 tablespoon olive oil, plus extra
   for greasing and brushing
½ tablespoon honey
375g strong white bread flour
1 teaspoon sea salt

Pour 250–300ml tepid water into a small bowl,
sprinkle in the yeast, add the olive oil and honey
and whisk with a fork until dissolved. Set aside.

Mix the flour and salt together in a large bowl.
Make a well in the centre and pour in the yeast
mixture. Bring together to form a soft dough, then
turn out onto a dusted work surface and knead
well for 10 minutes, until smooth and elastic.

Place the dough in a lightly greased large bowl
and brush the top with a little olive oil. Cover with
oiled cling film and leave the dough to rise in a
warm place for 45 minutes, or until doubled in
size. MAKES DOUGH FOR 4 PIZZAS

MOZZARELLA, ROASTED PEPPER AND CAPER PIZZA

polenta, for dusting
plain flour, for dusting
basic pizza dough (see recipe)
4 tablespoons passata
4 roasted red peppers in olive oil,
   drained and cut into wide strips
2 x 125g balls mozzarella cheese, sliced
2 tablespoons capers, drained
handful rocket leaves
extra-virgin olive oil, to drizzle

Preheat the oven to 250°C/gas mark 9 and dust
four 30cm pizza trays or two large oven trays with
polenta. Dust the work surface lightly with flour.
Turn out the pizza dough and knead for 1 minute
to knock back, then divide into 4 pieces. Cover with
oiled cling film and leave to rest for 15 minutes.

Flatten out one piece of dough into a rough circle
with the palm of your hand. Gently roll out to a
30cm circle and transfer to a prepared tray.

Spread 1 tablespoon passata onto the pizza base
with the back of a spoon and top with a quarter of
each topping – the peppers, mozzarella and capers.
Bake for 8–10 minutes, until the base is coloured
and crisp. Serve topped with rocket and a drizzle
of olive oil. MAKES 4 PIZZAS

Friday night is pizza night in the Granger household. I love pizza – crispy pizza with fresh toppings, rather than something slightly soggy that arrives in a cardboard box by motorbike. Scattering a little polenta over the pizza base is a simple trick to crisp it up.

BURRATA, PROSCIUTTO AND PEACH PIZZA

polenta, for dusting
plain flour, for dusting
basic pizza dough (see page 42)
extra-virgin olive oil, to drizzle
12 slices prosciutto
handful rocket leaves
2 x 125g burrata cheese
3 ripe peaches, stones removed and flesh torn

Preheat the oven to 250°C/gas mark 9 and dust four 30cm pizza trays or two large oven trays with polenta. Dust the work surface lightly with flour. Turn out the pizza dough and knead for 1 minute to knock back, then divide into 4 pieces. Cover with oiled cling film and leave to rest for 15 minutes.

Flatten out one piece of dough into a rough circle with the palm of your hand. Gently roll out to a 30cm circle and transfer to a prepared tray. Drizzle with the olive oil and bake each pizza, one at a time, for 6–10 minutes, or until the base is coloured and crisp. Top each pizza with a quarter each of the prosciutto, rocket, burrata and peaches and serve.
MAKES 4 PIZZAS

CARAMELISED FENNEL, FINOCCHIONA AND MOZZARELLA PIZZA

2 fennel bulbs, cut into wedges
1 orange, quartered
2 tablespoons olive oil, plus extra for drizzling
polenta, for dusting
plain flour, for dusting
basic pizza dough (see page 42)
2 x 125g balls mozzarella cheese, torn
60g black olives, pitted
6 slices finocchiona (fennel salami)
½ teaspoon dried chilli flakes

Preheat the oven to 250°C/gas mark 9. Place the fennel and orange wedges on a baking sheet and season with sea salt. Drizzle with olive oil and roast for 20–25 minutes, until softened and charred. Squeeze the juice from the orange wedges over the fennel and set aside to cool.

Dust four 30cm pizza trays or two large oven trays with polenta and dust the work surface lightly with flour. Turn out the pizza dough and knead for 1 minute to knock back, then divide into 4 pieces. Cover with oiled cling film and leave to rest for 15 minutes.

Flatten out one piece of dough into a rough circle with the palm of your hand. Gently roll out to a 30cm circle and transfer to a prepared tray. Add a quarter each of the mozzarella, olives and fennel and bake each pizza, one at a time, for 12–15 minutes, until the base is coloured and crisp. Top with the finocchiona and chilli flakes and serve. **MAKES 4 PIZZAS**

Local lore tells that finocchiona (fennel salami) was created when a

thief stole a salami and hid it away in a Tuscan field of wild fennel.

PLUM AND VANILLA COMPOTE

This is just the thing to make when stone fruit are in season and you've gone wild at the growers' market. Peaches and nectarines will work equally beautifully here. Serve with ice-cream or yoghurt, or on bread with mascarpone and an espresso chaser for an oh-so-stylish Italian breakfast. Or make a simple pastry and bake a teatime plum, vanilla and almond tart (page 243).

1kg ripe plums, halved and stones removed
pared zest and juice 2 oranges
80g caster sugar
1 vanilla pod, seeds scraped out and reserved

Place the plums and 125ml water in a large saucepan and heat over medium–low heat until the plums start to break down. Add the orange zest and juice, sugar and vanilla pod and seeds, and cook for 5 minutes. Remove from the heat and allow to cool to room temperature before spooning into sterilised jars. The compote will keep in the fridge for 1 week. MAKES 2 X 450G JARS

I have been told, many many times, that 'pronto' doesn't actually mean pronto in Italian. In fact, my Milanese friend assures me her family weep with laughter when they hear us English-speakers appropriate their word to mean quick and instant – because it's what real Italians say to answer the phone. But, for me, 'pronto' sums up all that is glorious about Italian dining: that a plate of cured meats and a salad of three simple but perfect ingredients can be on the table in a couple of fuss-free minutes ... Roughly the same length of time it takes me to find my mobile phone and answer the thing.

Pronto

INSTANT

MELON, PROSCIUTTO AND BURRATA SALAD

Burrata is a rich fresh cheese from Italy's Puglia region. At first glance it looks like a ball of mozzarella, but tear open the soft rind and you'll release the creamy curds inside. If you can't find burrata, rip up a ball of mozzarella and toss it with a couple of tablespoons of crème fraîche.

1 cantaloupe melon, deseeded
1 tablespoon extra-virgin olive oil,
   plus extra to serve
12 slices prosciutto
200g burrata cheese, torn
handful basil leaves, torn
handful rocket leaves, torn

Use a spoon to scoop out rough chunks of melon flesh into a bowl, catching any juice as you go. Add the olive oil and season with sea salt and freshly ground black pepper.

Divide the dressed melon and the prosciutto between four plates. Top with the burrata, basil and rocket and a grinding of black pepper. Drizzle lightly with olive oil and serve. SERVES 4

One of the most refreshingly relaxing aspects of a holiday in Italy for me is that any meal can consist of a plate of antipasto, or a couple of salads and some simply grilled meats. I've tried to stick with this idea since I've been home – although I suspect that if you live in a house bursting with teenagers you will need to add bread into this equation.

RAW COURGETTE, ROCKET AND RICOTTA PASTA SALAD

300g dried short pasta shape, such as
   fusilli, penne or garganelle
juice and zest 1 lemon
3 tablespoons olive oil
2 garlic cloves, crushed
3 courgettes, sliced
250g rocket leaves
250g ricotta cheese
extra-virgin olive oil, to drizzle
½ teaspoon dried chilli flakes

Cook the pasta in a large saucepan of salted boiling water according to the instructions on the packet, until al dente. Drain, refresh under running water and drain again.

Mix the lemon juice and zest with the oil and garlic then pour over the pasta. Stir in the courgette and rocket and place on a serving dish. Dot with the ricotta, give the salad a good drizzle of extra-virgin olive oil and sprinkle with chilli flakes. SERVES 4

ORANGE, FENNEL AND DILL SALAD

1 red chilli, deseeded and chopped
1 garlic clove, crushed
3 tablespoons olive oil
2 oranges, peeled, pith left on
2 fennel bulbs, thinly sliced
large handful dill, chopped
large handful mint, chopped

In a large bowl combine the chilli, garlic and olive oil. Thinly slice the oranges over the bowl to catch any juice. Add the orange slices, fennel, dill and mint to the bowl and season with sea salt and freshly ground black pepper. Gently toss, trying not to break up the oranges too much, and serve. SERVES 4

The looseness of the Italian dining table, with platters to pass and

share, seems perfectly designed to create a friendly stress-free meal.

PEAR, SPECK AND RADICCHIO SALAD

If you happen to have chestnut honey in your pantry (and who doesn't?), this is the time to use it. Otherwise, ordinary runny honey is fine.

2 pears, cut into wedges and cored
juice ½ lemon
1 shallot, finely sliced
1 tablespoon honey
2 tablespoons extra-virgin olive oil,
   plus extra to serve
1 head radicchio, broken into leaves
12 slices speck
250g goat's cheese, crumbled
   or broken into chunks
60g roasted walnuts

In a large bowl toss the pears with the lemon juice. Mix together the shallot, honey and olive oil. Add to the pears with some sea salt and gently combine. Toss in the radicchio and transfer to a large platter.

Drape the speck over the salad and dot with the goat's cheese. Crush the walnuts over the top with your hands and drizzle with olive oil. **SERVES 4**

ASPARAGUS AND POACHED EGG SALAD

I love raw vegetables, so when asparagus are at their slim green best I just slice them wafer-thin and don't even bother to blanch – marinating in the lemony dressing is enough to soften them slightly. (Remember: 'wafer-thin' though, or they could be woody.) This beautiful combination of flavours and textures makes a perfect light dinner.

200g asparagus, sliced into thin lengths
1 shallot, finely chopped
juice 1 lemon
3 tablespoons extra-virgin olive oil
4 very fresh free-range eggs
large handful rocket leaves
¼ teaspoon dried chilli flakes
25g fresh parmesan cheese shavings

Blanch the asparagus for 1 minute in boiling water and drain. Mix together the shallot, lemon juice and oil with sea salt and freshly ground black pepper. Add the asparagus and toss to coat. Set aside.

In a shallow frying pan, bring 5cm of water to the boil. Turn off the heat and add the eggs at once. To minimise the spreading of the whites, break the eggs directly into the water, carefully opening the two halves of the shells at the water surface so they slide into the water. Cover the pan with a tight-fitting lid and leave them to cook undisturbed for about 3 minutes. The eggs are cooked when the whites are opaque. Remove from the pan with a slotted spoon and drain on a clean tea towel.

Toss the rocket into the asparagus and divide between four plates. Top each with a poached egg and any remaining dressing. Scatter with the chilli flakes and parmesan shavings and serve. **SERVES 4**

MOZZARELLA AND RED PEPPER TOASTS

2 large eggs
2 tablespoons milk
125g mozzarella cheese, sliced
4 slices crusty bread
1 roasted red pepper in olive oil,
   drained and cut into thick strips
4 basil leaves, torn
2 teaspoons capers, drained
4 tablespoons olive oil

Lightly beat the eggs and milk in a shallow bowl and season with sea salt and freshly ground black pepper. Divide the mozzarella between two bread slices and add the pepper strips, basil and capers. Top with a second slice of bread to make two sandwiches and press down firmly to flatten them.

Dip the sandwiches in the seasoned egg, making sure they are well coated on both sides. Heat half the oil in a large frying pan over medium heat and fry a sandwich for 4–5 minutes on each side, until golden and crisp. Repeat with the remaining oil and sandwich. Eat while they're still warm. **MAKES 2**

MORTADELLA, ASIAGO AND OLIVE PANINI

The sandwich press is king in our house at the moment. We bought ours recently and are at the over-excited stage when we use it every day – for every meal. These panini are easy enough to make in a frying pan but, if you have a press, let it work its magic here.

4 slices crusty bread
1 tablespoon black olive paste
125g asiago cheese, sliced
4 slices mortadella
olive oil, to drizzle

Spread two slices of bread with the olive paste and top with the asiago and mortadella. Cover with the remaining bread slices to make two sandwiches.

Lightly drizzle the sandwiches with olive oil and toast in a hot frying pan or on a griddle for 1–2 minutes on each side, pressing down firmly with a metal spatula so the bread crisps up and becomes golden. Serve immediately. **MAKES 2**

ARTICHOKE, CRISPY PROSCIUTTO AND MINT BRUSCHETTE

small handful mint leaves
1 garlic clove, sliced
2 tablespoons olive oil, plus extra to drizzle
4 slices crusty bread
4 slices prosciutto
280g jar artichokes in olive oil, drained

Mix together the mint, garlic and 2 tablespoons olive oil. Set aside.

Preheat the grill to high. Place the slices of bread on a baking sheet and lightly drizzle with olive oil. Grill on both sides until toasted and golden. Remove and set aside. Place the prosciutto in a single layer on the baking sheet and grill for 5 minutes, until crisp.

Halve the artichokes and divide them between the toasted bread slices. Top with the crispy prosciutto and the mint and garlic to serve. MAKES 4

TALEGGIO AND SPECK BRUSCHETTE

4 slices crusty bread
olive oil, for drizzling
220g taleggio cheese, sliced
8 slices speck

Preheat the grill to high. Place the slices of bread on a baking sheet and lightly drizzle with olive oil. Grill on both sides until toasted and golden.

Top with the taleggio and speck and add a good grinding of black pepper to serve. MAKES 4

MOZZARELLA, FENNEL AND LEMON BRUSCHETTE

2 teaspoons fennel seeds
4 slices crusty bread
olive oil, for drizzling
250g mozzarella cheese, torn
zest ½ lemon

Toast the fennel seeds in a dry pan, until they start to release their aroma.

Preheat the grill to high. Place the slices of bread on a baking sheet and lightly drizzle with olive oil. Grill on both sides until toasted and golden.

Top the toasts with mozzarella and scatter with the fennel seeds, lemon zest and a drizzle of olive oil. Season with sea salt and serve. MAKES 4

SPAGHETTI AND HERB FRITTATA

What a great 'next day dinner' for using up cooked pasta. I've resolved never again to leave a silly quarter-full bag of pasta in the cupboard ... I'll cook the whole packet and make this with the leftovers.

5 eggs, lightly beaten
100ml milk
handful rocket leaves
handful baby spinach leaves
2 tablespoons olive oil
1 large onion, sliced
½ teaspoon dried chilli flakes (optional)
500g cold leftover cooked spaghetti
    (cooked weight)
sliced tomatoes dressed with olive oil
    and marjoram, to serve

Preheat the grill to high. Combine the egg and milk in a large bowl and season with sea salt and freshly ground black pepper. Stir in the rocket and spinach leaves and set aside.

Heat the oil in a large non-stick frying pan over medium–high heat. Add the onion and chilli flakes and cook for 8 minutes, until softened and turning golden. Add the pasta and toss, as if stir-frying, until the pasta starts to look lightly toasted. Tip the pasta into the bowl with the eggs and leaves, toss well to combine, then tip the mixture into the pan and quickly level out the pasta.

Reduce the heat a little and cook for 6–8 minutes, until the base is set. Place the frying pan under the hot grill for a few minutes to cook the top. Slice and serve with the dressed tomatoes. **SERVES 4**

ONION AND GOAT'S CHEESE FRITTATA

15g butter, plus a knob extra
1 tablespoon olive oil
2 onions, sliced
2 garlic cloves, crushed
1 tablespoon thyme leaves
6 eggs
125g soft rindless goat's cheese
handful flat-leaf parsley, leaves picked

Heat 15g butter and the oil in a large non-stick frying pan over medium–high heat. Tip in the onion and cook for 10 minutes, stirring regularly, until soft and deeply caramelised. Add the garlic and thyme and cook for a further minute. Remove and set aside.

In a bowl beat the eggs with some sea salt and freshly ground black pepper, until smooth. Wipe out the frying pan and heat the knob of butter. Once foaming, pour in the beaten egg and cook for 4 minutes, until the base is set. Spoon over the caramelised onions and dot with the goat's cheese. Cook for further 1–2 minutes, until the egg has just set and the cheese has melted. Add a grinding of black pepper and scatter with the parsley to serve.
SERVES 4

TORN PASTA, BUTTER AND PARMESAN

280g bought fresh lasagne sheets
60g butter
80g parmesan cheese, grated

Tear the lasagne sheets into random-sized pieces
and cook in a large saucepan of boiling salted
water, until al dente. Drain, reserving a little of
the cooking water.

Return the pasta to the pan, add the butter
and parmesan, and stir over medium–high heat
to combine. Add a little of the pasta water and
continue to stir to form a creamy coating. Season
with lots of sea salt and freshly ground black
pepper and serve. SERVES 2, OR 4 AS A STARTER

FRIED RAVIOLI AND SAGE BUTTER

I add capers to this Italian classic to cut through
the richness of the butter. This is a great way to
give texture to bought ravioli – let them catch on
the pan bottom until they're browned and crunchy.

500g bought fresh spinach and ricotta ravioli
80g butter
2 tablespoons olive oil
handful sage leaves
1 tablespoon capers, drained

Cook the ravioli in a large pan of boiling salted
water, until al dente. Drain.

Heat the butter and olive oil in a large non-stick
frying pan. When foaming add the sage and capers
and fry for 1–2 minutes, until the sage is crisp.
Remove with a slotted spoon and set aside.

Return the pan to the heat, tip in the ravioli and fry
for 2–3 minutes, until starting to colour. Divide the
ravioli between four plates, top with the capers and
fried sage and any butter left in the pan. SERVES 4

SPICY SPAGHETTI

Hungry, but nothing in the fridge? Here's the clever
solution. And, if you've a tin of tuna and a bunch of
rocket, throw them in for a perfect instant supper.

375g spaghetti
4 tablespoons olive oil
4 garlic cloves, sliced
2–3 teaspoons dried chilli flakes

Cook the spaghetti in a large saucepan of salted
boiling water according to the instructions on the
packet, until al dente.

Meanwhile, heat the olive oil in a large frying pan.
Add the garlic and chilli flakes and let sizzle for
1–2 minutes, stirring frequently. If the garlic starts
to colour too much, remove the pan from the heat.

Drain the spaghetti, toss into the frying pan to
combine and serve. SERVES 4

Trofie is the traditional pasta of Liguria. These long thin twists were apparently hand-rolled by fishermen's wives on their knees while they waited for their men to sail home. It doesn't really matter which pasta shape you use here (or which part of your body you like to roll it on).

TROFIE, AUBERGINE, CHERRY TOMATOES AND PECORINO

The soft goat's cheese coats the pasta and gives this dish its creaminess. You could use any soft cheese to do the same job, even fresh ricotta.

2 aubergines, sliced
3 tablespoons olive oil
250g cherry tomatoes
2 garlic cloves, sliced
1 red chilli, thinly sliced
350g trofie
35g pecorino romano cheese, grated
35g parmesan cheese, freshly grated,
   plus extra to serve
100g soft goat's cheese
10 large basil leaves, torn

Coat the aubergine in 1 tablespoon olive oil and cook them on a hot griddle over high heat for 5 minutes on each side, until charred and tender.

Heat the remaining oil in a large heavy-based frying pan over medium–high heat. Add the tomatoes and when they begin to blister, stir in the garlic and chilli. Fry for a further minute then stir in the aubergine. Set aside.

Cook the pasta in a large pan of salted boiling water according to the instructions on the packet, until al dente. Drain, reserving a ladleful of the cooking water. Tip the pasta into the frying pan with the vegetables and toss until well coated and velvety. Add the reserved cooking water and continue stirring until absorbed. Stir in the pecorino and parmesan. Serve dotted with dollops of the goat's cheese, basil leaves and extra parmesan.

SERVES 4

ORECCHIETTE, SPROUTING BROCCOLI AND CHILLI

350g dried orecchiette
350g sprouting broccoli, roughly chopped
30g butter
5 tablespoons olive oil
½ teaspoon dried chilli flakes
2 garlic cloves, crushed
90g fine fresh breadcrumbs
freshly grated parmesan cheese, to serve

Bring a large saucepan of salted water to the boil. Tip in the orecchiette and broccoli and cook the pasta according to the instructions on the packet, until al dente. Drain.

While the pasta is cooking, heat the butter and 1 tablespoon of the olive oil in a large frying pan over medium heat. When the butter has melted and starts sizzling, stir in the chilli flakes and half the garlic. Tip in the breadcrumbs and fry, stirring, until golden. Transfer to a plate and return the pan to the heat.

Heat the remaining oil and garlic over high heat. Stir for a few seconds, then add the drained pasta and toss until well coated, breaking up the broccoli. Serve scattered with the golden breadcrumbs and parmesan. **SERVES 4**

I tend to blanch vegetables very briefly, so they keep a bit of 'bite'. However, this dish works best when the broccoli is cooked until completely soft (and throwing it in with the pasta saves you dirtying another pan). The toasted golden breadcrumbs provide the crunch here.

Just like a lot of other family cooks, I get stuck in the weekday rut of recycling the same (predictable, and slightly tired) dinners month after month. When I see how Italian families eat together, I always vow I'm never going to 'cook boring' at home again. So, there are no reworkings of spaghetti bolognese or fish fingers here. What I'm aiming for is a simple trattoria menu of ideas that will hopefully bring a little bit of magic back into all our weekday kitchens. (Although, having watched small Italian children drinking espresso, I've realised that there are limits to how far I want to ramp up the excitement.)

famiglia
WEEKDAY

RICE AND PEA SOUP

30g butter
1 tablespoon olive oil
1 onion, chopped
1 garlic clove, crushed
250g arborio rice
1.25 litres chicken stock
400g peas (fresh or frozen)
handful mint leaves, roughly chopped
80g parmesan cheese, freshly grated
2 x 125g balls mozzarella cheese, drained and torn
extra-virgin olive oil, to serve

Heat the butter and oil in a large heavy-based saucepan over medium–low heat. When the butter has melted, add the onion and cook for 8 minutes, until soft. Add the garlic, cook for another minute, then stir in the rice and stock.

Increase the heat and bring to the boil, then simmer for 18 minutes, until the rice is just cooked. Add the peas and continue to cook for 5 minutes, until the rice is very tender and the peas are soft.

Remove from the heat, stir in the mint and half the parmesan and season with sea salt and freshly ground black pepper. Ladle into bowls and top with torn mozzarella, the remaining parmesan and a drizzle of extra-virgin olive oil. SERVES 4

CHICKEN AND PANCETTA MEATBALLS IN KALE BROTH

1 tablespoon olive oil
1 onion, finely diced
75g sliced pancetta, finely chopped
1 tablespoon finely chopped rosemary,
    plus 1 sprig
6 sage leaves, finely chopped
3 tablespoons freshly grated parmesan cheese,
    plus extra to serve
400g chicken mince
35g fresh white breadcrumbs
1 egg white, lightly beaten
1.75 litres chicken stock
1 bay leaf
1 courgette, cut into chunks
300g winter leaves, such as kale, cavolo nero
    or savoy cabbage, tough stalks removed
    and cut into pieces

Heat the olive oil in a large, heavy-based frying pan. Add the onion and pancetta and cook for 8 minutes, or until the onion is soft and the pancetta is starting to crisp. Add the chopped rosemary and sage leaves and continue to cook for 1 minute. Remove from the heat and transfer to a large mixing bowl to cool.

Add the parmesan, mince and breadcrumbs and combine. Gradually add the egg white and squeeze the mixture with your hands, until well combined. Add more breadcrumbs if the mixture feels too wet; extra egg white if too dry. Wet your hands to form the mixture into walnut-sized balls, and place on a lined tray and chill until ready to cook.

Pour the chicken stock into a large saucepan and slowly bring to the boil with the rosemary sprig and bay leaf. Lower the meatballs into the broth and cook for 10 minutes, skimming the broth occasionally to ensure it is clear. Add the courgette and winter leaves and cook for a further 6–7 minutes, until they are tender but still vibrant green. Ladle into large soup bowls and finish with freshly grated parmesan cheese. SERVES 4

If you're going to serve soup for a main course, then it needs to be pretty substantial (it does in my house anyway). Rice and pea soup (*risi e bisi*) has to be the ultimate 'empty pantry' dinner trick. The chicken meatballs are a lovely (and lighter) alternative to red meat and you can pack the soup with more vegies if you need to stretch it a little further.

TOMATO, CHILLI AND MUSSEL SOUP

Mussels are something I don't tend to choose mid-week, but I have no idea why! They're not expensive and are quick to cook, especially now we can buy them cleaned from the supermarket. Use sweet, ripe tomatoes here; I like to mix a few varieties of different shapes and colours.

1.5kg mixed tomatoes, large ones halved
small bunch thyme
3 tablespoons olive oil
3 shallots, chopped
1 fennel, thinly sliced, fronds reserved
2 garlic cloves, thinly sliced
2 red chillies, chopped
400g tin diced tomatoes
180ml dry white wine
1kg mussels, de-bearded and scrubbed
500ml fish stock, heated

Preheat the oven to 220°C/gas mark 7. Place the fresh tomatoes in a large roasting tin and scatter with the thyme. Drizzle with 2 tablespoons olive oil and season with sea salt. Roast for 20–25 minutes, until soft and juicy.

Heat 1 tablespoon olive oil in a large saucepan with a lid, over medium heat. Add the shallots, sliced fennel, garlic and chilli and cook for 5 minutes. Tip in the tinned tomatoes, wine and half the roasted tomatoes and simmer gently for 5 minutes. Increase the heat to high and add the mussels. Cover with the lid, shake the pan and allow to steam for 3 minutes, or until the mussels open. Discard any that do not open. Pour in the hot fish stock, gently fold through the remaining roasted tomatoes and serve topped with the fennel fronds.
SERVES 4

My daughter Inès loves this bake so much that it's become a bit of a joke in our house – she would eat it every night if she was allowed. But it's quick, tasty and healthy so I haven't been complaining. In fact, dinner's ready, sweetie ...

TOMATO AND MOZZARELLA GNOCCHI BAKE

This is a great crowd-pleaser and a lovely way to serve bought gnocchi. If you've taken the time to make your own beautiful silky potato gnocchi, step away from this recipe and serve it simply with butter and fried sage leaves.

500g gnocchi
5 basil leaves, torn
2 x 125g balls mozzarella cheese, torn
2 tablespoons freshly grated parmesan cheese
1 tablespoon olive oil
for the tomato sauce
400g tin diced tomatoes
1 garlic clove, crushed
1 tablespoon olive oil

Preheat the oven to 200°C/gas mark 6. Make the tomato sauce by heating the tomatoes in a saucepan and simmering for 2 minutes. Remove from the heat and stir in the garlic and olive oil. Season with sea salt and set aside.

Cook the gnocchi in a large pan of salted boiling water for 2 minutes, until they float to the top of the pan. Drain and stir in the tomato sauce and basil. Tip into an ovenproof dish and top with the mozzarella and parmesan. Drizzle with olive oil and bake for 15–20 minutes, or until the mozzarella has melted and the sauce is bubbling. **SERVES 4**

BAKED POLENTA, FRIED MUSHROOMS, DOLCELATTE AND WALNUTS

250g instant polenta
50g butter
3 tablespoons freshly grated parmesan cheese
1 tablespoon olive oil, plus extra for greasing
500g mixed wild and cultivated mushrooms, thickly sliced
3 garlic cloves, finely chopped
2 tablespoons thyme leaves
150g dolcelatte cheese, torn
50g roasted walnuts, chopped
lemon wedges, to serve
rocket dressed with olive oil and balsamic vinegar, to serve

Make the polenta by stirring it into boiling water, according to the instructions on the packet. Once it's ready, add half the butter, the parmesan and plenty of sea salt and freshly ground black pepper. Stir well until the butter has melted. Pour into a lightly oiled frying pan and spread out with the back of a spoon to get an even layer. Leave to set.

Preheat the oven to 180°C/gas mark 4. Put the pan of cooled polenta over medium–high heat and cook until the base of the polenta is crisp and golden. Transfer to the oven to heat through while you cook the mushrooms.

Heat the remaining butter and the olive oil in a large, non-stick frying pan over high heat, until the butter starts to sizzle. Add the mushrooms and cook, stirring, until softened and golden. Reduce the heat and add the garlic and thyme. Cook for a further minute.

Turn the polenta out onto a plate. Slice into wedges and serve topped with the mushrooms, dolcelatte, walnuts, a squeeze of lemon juice and a handful of dressed rocket leaves. SERVES 4

CHICKEN, GREEN OLIVES, PINE NUTS AND GARLIC

2 tablespoons olive oil
4 chicken legs, thighs and drumsticks separated
10 shallots, peeled
4 garlic cloves, sliced
2 bay leaves
150ml dry white wine
1 tablespoon white wine vinegar
1 teaspoon soft brown sugar
300ml chicken stock
100g green olives
50g toasted pine nuts
handful flat-leaf parsley, roughly chopped

Heat the oil in a large shallow casserole dish over medium–high heat. Season the chicken with sea salt and freshly ground black pepper and brown the pieces all over for 15 minutes, or until golden brown. Add the shallots and cook for 2–3 minutes, turning them occasionally until they start taking on some colour. Add the garlic, bay leaves and wine. Let bubble for a few minutes and scrape the bottom of the pan to collect up the flavours. Pour in the vinegar, sugar, stock and olives. Bring to the boil then partially cover and simmer for 45 minutes, or until the chicken is very tender. Scatter over the pine nuts and parsley before serving. SERVES 4

GRILLED LAMB CUTLETS AND BROAD BEANS

A little while ago we went through a craze for 'frenching' the bones of lamb cutlets – scraping them clean so they looked like beautiful little bleached handles. I actually prefer my cutlets with the meat on the bones so we all have something to gnaw at the end of the meal. Call me uncouth ...

for the broad beans
440g broad beans (podded weight)
1 garlic clove, chopped
zest 1 orange, plus squeeze of juice
small bunch tarragon, leaves picked and chopped
handful mint, roughly chopped
extra-virgin olive oil, to drizzle
50g roasted hazelnuts, roughly chopped
for the lamb cutlets
8 lamb cutlets
2 teaspoons olive oil
1 teaspoon dried chilli flakes
½ teaspoon sea salt

Cook the broad beans in boiling salted water for 5 minutes, or until tender. Drain and refresh in cold water. Drain again and tip into a bowl with the garlic, orange zest and a squeeze of juice. Stir in the tarragon, mint and lots of sea salt and freshly ground black pepper, then add a generous drizzle of olive oil. Fold through the hazelnuts and set aside.

Rub the cutlets with the oil. Pound the chilli flakes and salt to a rough powder and sprinkle over the lamb. Heat a griddle pan over high heat and cook for 2 minutes on each side. Remove from the pan and serve with the broad beans. SERVES 4

PAN-FRIED SEA BASS, CAPERS AND LEMON

2 tablespoons olive oil
4 sea bass fillets (about 150g each), skin on
2 tablespoons capers, drained
1 garlic clove, thinly sliced
½ lemon, thinly sliced
green bean and little gem salad
   (see recipe), to serve

Heat 1 tablespoon oil in a large non-stick frying
pan over medium heat. Season the fillets with sea
salt and freshly ground black pepper and cook,
skin side down, for 2–3 minutes, until the skin is
crisp and golden. Turn over and cook for one further
minute then remove to a platter and keep warm.

Return the pan to the heat, turn up the temperature
and heat the remaining oil. Tip in the capers, garlic
and lemon slices and sizzle until the capers burst
open and look crisp. Spoon over the sea bass and
serve with green bean and little gem salad. SERVES 4

GREEN BEAN AND LITTLE GEM SALAD

2 tablespoons extra-virgin olive oil
juice 1 lemon
1 garlic clove, crushed
200g green beans, trimmed
handful mint leaves, chopped
2 little gem lettuces, leaves separated and halved

Mix together the oil, lemon juice and garlic and
season with sea salt and freshly ground black
pepper. Cook the beans in a saucepan of boiling
water for 2 minutes, then drain and toss in the
dressing. Allow the beans to cool, then toss in
the mint and lettuce leaves and serve. SERVES 4

ROASTED SALMON, ASPARAGUS AND PANCETTA WITH CAPER AND BASIL MAYO

The eagle-eyed Italophiles among you will notice
that this isn't an entirely Italian-looking dish. But
a piece of crisp-skinned salmon is one of my
favourite weekday dinners, so here it is, sneaking
in after a Dolce & Gabbana makeover.

1 tablespoon capers, drained
8 basil leaves, roughly chopped
juice ½ lemon, plus wedges, to serve
5 tablespoons good-quality mayonnaise
4 salmon fillets (about 175g each), skin on
250g asparagus, halved length and widthways
8 slices prosciutto
2 tablespoons olive oil

Preheat the oven to 220°C/gas mark 7. Stir the
capers, basil and lemon juice into the mayonnaise.
Season with sea salt and freshly ground black
pepper and set aside.

Place the salmon (skin side up), asparagus and
prosciutto slices in a roasting tin large enough
to fit them comfortably in a single layer. Add salt
and pepper and drizzle with the olive oil. Roast for
10 minutes, until the salmon is just cooked, the
pancetta is crisp and the asparagus charred. Serve
with the mayonnaise and lemon wedges. SERVES 4

ITALIAN SAUSAGE AND CHIPS

500g good-quality coarse pork sausages
500g new potatoes, quartered
1 tablespoon olive oil
½ teaspoon dried chilli flakes
1 tablespoon fennel seeds
4 rosemary sprigs
8 garlic cloves, unpeeled and bashed
200ml dry white wine
torn tomato sauce (see recipe), to serve

Preheat the oven to 200°C/gas mark 6. Toss all the ingredients except the wine together in a large roasting tin. Season with sea salt and freshly ground black pepper and roast for 20 minutes. Pour in the wine and give everything a good stir. Return to the oven for a further 20–30 minutes, until the sausage is cooked, the potatoes are golden and the wine has made a sticky sauce at the bottom of the tray. Serve with torn tomato sauce. **SERVES 4**

TORN TOMATO SAUCE

400g ripe cherry tomatoes, halved
½ teaspoon sea salt
1 garlic clove, crushed
1 tablespoon red wine vinegar
½ teaspoon caster sugar
1 tablespoon olive oil

Preheat the oven to 200°C/gas mark 6. Spread the tomatoes in a single layer on a baking sheet and sprinkle with the salt. Cook for 30 minutes, or until slightly shrivelled and looking a little dry. Tip into a bowl, add the garlic, vinegar, sugar and olive oil and mash lightly with a fork. Allow to cool to room temperature before serving. **SERVES 4**

I love the Italian-style coarse meat pork sausages, both for sausage

and chips, and also as the filling for these stuffed roasted peppers.

CRISPY CHICKEN UNDER A BRICK

Traditionally, the chicken is weighted down with a brick to keep it flat during cooking. This gives it a crisp charred skin while keeping the meat succulent. Using a pan of water is a clever alternative. I wish I'd thought of it the first time I made this, when I was an earnest 18 year old and dragged a landscaping rock from the garden into my mother's kitchen. Being a typical teenage boy, I didn't even bother to put it back when I'd finished.

1 small chicken (about 1.25kg)
1 lemon
1 tablespoon olive oil
1 tablespoon chopped rosemary
cauliflower and fennel salad (see recipe), to serve

Start by spatchcocking the chicken. Lay it breast side down and with a pair of strong kitchen shears cut along the back about 0.5cm from either side of the backbone, starting at the neck end; you'll then be able to remove the backbone easily. Turn the chicken over and flatten it by pressing down firmly on the breast with the palm of your hand, until you hear the breastbone crack. Place on a large plate and squeeze the lemon juice over it. Set aside for 15 minutes.

Fill a large saucepan with water. Rub the chicken with the oil and season with sea salt and freshly ground black pepper. Heat a large heavy-based frying pan over high heat. Add the chicken, skin side down, and immediately sit the saucepan full of water on top, to weigh down and flatten the chicken. Reduce the heat to medium and cook for 15 minutes. Turn the chicken over, weigh it down again and cook for a further 15 minutes. Scatter the rosemary all over the chicken and turn it over to lay skin side down once again. Cover with the saucepan and cook for a final 10–15 minutes, until cooked through, with no signs of pink. Allow to rest for 5 minutes then serve with the cauliflower and fennel salad. SERVES 4

CAULIFLOWER AND FENNEL SALAD

4 tablespoons extra-virgin olive oil
1½ tablespoons white wine vinegar
½ teaspoon caster sugar
2 tablespoons capers, drained
2 anchovy fillets, chopped
1 shallot, very finely diced
1 fennel bulb, tough outer leaves and base of core removed, fronds reserved
2 celery sticks
1 head cauliflower, broken into florets
handful roasted pistachios, chopped

To make the dressing, mix the olive oil, vinegar and sugar in a large bowl and stir until the sugar has dissolved. Add the capers, anchovies and shallot and set aside while you prepare the vegetables.

Use a mandolin to thinly slice the fennel, celery and cauliflower florets. Toss into the dressing with the pistachios and season with sea salt and freshly ground black pepper. Scatter with the fennel fronds before serving. SERVES 4

I can remember my mother serving stuffed peppers when I was a child; they were very much a dish of that time. Having eaten them again in Italy, I wonder why they went out of fashion for the rest of us. They are simple to make and absolutely delicious. For my 'modern' version, I chop my ingredients a little coarser and tear the bread into chunks rather than making crumbs, so the filling keeps some texture.

STUFFED PEPPERS WITH SAUSAGE, HERBS AND TORN BREAD

6 good-quality coarse pork sausages,
  meat squeezed out of skins in pieces
100g cherry tomatoes
1 onion, chopped
handful rosemary leaves, roughly chopped
handful thyme sprigs, roughly chopped
¼ teaspoon dried chilli flakes
2 garlic cloves, sliced
2 tablespoons olive oil
4 large red peppers, halved and deseeded
2 slices rustic bread, torn into chunks

Preheat the oven to 200°C/gas mark 6. Mix the sausage pieces, cherry tomatoes, onion and herbs in a large bowl. Add the chilli, garlic, oil and some salt and toss well to combine. Put the peppers, cut-side up, on a baking tray and loosely fill them with the sausage mixture. Cook for 45 minutes–1 hour, until the filling looks golden and the peppers tender.

Tear the bread into large chunks and push the pieces into any gaps between the peppers, to soak up the juices. Return to the oven for 10 minutes, or until the bread is toasted and golden. SERVES 4

SPINACH AND MASCARPONE TART

Baby spinach leaves are quick and easy to use here (especially if they come ready-washed and bagged), but you can get great flavour from large leaf spinach when it's in season. You can also use Swiss chard, but do cut away the tough stalks from the leaves when you wash them. Bought puff pastry makes this a very easy dinner.

375g puff pastry
1 tablespoon olive oil
2 garlic cloves, sliced
400g baby spinach leaves
freshly grated nutmeg
2 medium eggs, beaten
250g mascarpone cheese
80g parmesan cheese, freshly grated
pinch dried chilli flakes (optional)

Preheat the oven to 200°C/gas mark 6. Line a 20cm x 30cm shallow baking tin with greaseproof paper. Roll out the pastry so that it fits into the tin, pushing it into the corners and up the sides. Cover with a scrunched up piece of baking paper, line with baking beans and bake for 15 minutes. Remove from the oven, tip out the baking beans and paper and bake for a further 10 minutes, until the pastry is golden and crisp. Leave the oven on.

Heat the oil in a large non-stick frying pan over high heat. Add the garlic and, after a few seconds, the spinach. Cook, stirring, for 1–2 minutes, until wilted then add a grating of nutmeg and stir well. Drain on kitchen paper to remove any excess water.

Mix together the egg, mascarpone and most of the parmesan and pour into the pastry shell. Dot over the cooked spinach and sprinkle with the remaining parmesan and the chilli, if using. Bake for 25–30 minutes, until the filling is just set. Allow to cool for a few minutes before slicing and serving.
SERVES 4

SAUSAGE AND BROCCOLI BUNS

2 tablespoons olive oil
4 garlic cloves, sliced
½ teaspoon dried chilli flakes
400g sprouting broccoli, halved
180ml chicken stock
grated zest ½ lemon
8 good-quality coarse pork sausages
4 bread rolls

Heat the oil in a large deep-sided frying pan over
medium heat. Add the garlic and chilli flakes and
cook until the garlic is starting to colour. Add the
broccoli, season with sea salt and freshly ground
black pepper and stir to coat in the garlic and chilli.
Pour in the stock and bring to the boil, then cover
and simmer for 12–15 minutes, until the broccoli
is very soft and almost falling apart and the liquid
is clinging to it. Add the lemon zest and extra salt,
if needed. Stir through and remove from the heat.

Heat a barbecue or oven grill to high. Cook the
sausages for 15–20 minutes, depending on their
thickness, until brown and cooked through. Split
the buns open and toast them slightly, then fill
with the sausages and broccoli. SERVES 4

The 'sausage sizzle' is a much-loved Australian school special, served at welcome evenings, fetes and fund-raisers. The snags are barbecued by a team of sun-broiled but smiling parents, then wrapped in slices of white bread. It's an Atussie tradition, but I recognise it does miss out a few vital food groups. (It took a while to convince my girls that a squirt of tomato sauce does not constitute a 'vegetable'.) For an at-home weekday sausage sizzle this is an entire meal in a bun. If you need to disguise the greenery, ketchup should do the trick ... organic, of course!

Con calma means 'slow down' for us non-Italian speakers. Anyone who's been to Italy will know that it's the home of the slow cooking movement. They'll also have realised that timekeeping doesn't play an important role in the Italian lifestyle. Italians don't rush; they would rather arrive late (sometimes very late!) than get themselves flustered and sweaty. That might drive us crazy while we acclimatise, but it's a lovely reminder to slow down and smell the espresso in our crazy logged-on world. None of these recipes is slow in Italian terms, but they're a little more lazily paced than my usual weekday fare.

Con Calma
SLOW

ARTICHOKE AND HAM LASAGNE

680ml bottle passata
315g fresh lasagne sheets
220g sliced good-quality cooked ham
3 x 125g balls mozzarella cheese, torn
3 tablespoons freshly grated parmesan cheese
430g jar artichokes in olive oil,
  drained and halved

Preheat the oven to 200°C/gas mark 7.

To assemble the lasagne, season the passata with sea salt and spoon a small amount into the base of a 20cm x 30cm ovenproof dish. Cover with a layer of lasagne sheets, quickly dipping the sheets in a bowl of cold water first before using them. Spoon over one-third of the remaining passata, then half the ham slices, 1 of the mozzarellas and 1 tablespoon parmesan. Cover with another layer of dipped lasagne sheets then top with half the remaining passata, all the ham, 1 mozzarella and 1 tablespoon parmesan. Add the final layer of lasagne sheets. Scatter the artichokes over the top and spoon over the last of the passata, mozzarella and parmesan. Bake for 30 minutes, or until the cheese is bubbling and golden. SERVES 4–6

By the time I've bolognesed, béchameled and layered, I find traditional lasagne requires an entire Sunday afternoon to complete. I love the whole process when I'm in the mood, but I'm also a fan of the short cut – and this is a short cut that, I think, surpasses the original. The flavours are inspired by ham and artichoke pizza. You could use thin slices of prosciutto crudo here (such as Parma ham or San Daniele), but I prefer cooked ham (sold as 'prosciutto cotto' in Italy).

There is not a drop of Granger Italian blood. My only (admittedly rather tenuous) claim to any Italian cultural sensibilities is that my grandfather was a big fan of lamb neck. As a butcher, he found it incomprehensible that this well-priced cut of meat, beautifully tender when cooked slowly, was often unsold when the shop shut.

BRAISED LAMB NECK

1 tablespoon olive oil
1kg lamb neck fillet, cut into 5cm lengths
1 onion, diced
1 fennel bulb, cut into wedges
2 garlic cloves, chopped
2 rosemary sprigs
1 bay leaf
180ml dry white wine
250ml chicken stock
wet polenta (see recipe)
handful flat-leaf parsley, to serve
grated zest 1 lemon, to serve

Preheat the oven to 160°C/gas mark 3. Heat the oil in a large shallow casserole dish over medium–high heat. Season the lamb with sea salt and freshly ground black pepper and cook in batches, until well browned. Remove from the pan and set aside.

Tip in the onion and fennel and cook until starting to colour. Add the garlic and cook for 30 seconds. Return the lamb to the casserole dish, also adding the rosemary and bay leaf. Pour in the wine and boil for 1 minute to cook off the alcohol. Pour in the stock and bring to the boil, then cover and transfer the dish to the oven. Cook for 2 hours, or until the lamb is very tender. Remove from the oven and season with salt and pepper. Serve over wet polenta, scattered with parsley and lemon zest. **SERVES 4**

WET POLENTA

Italy's smoothest, creamiest polenta is found in the Veneto. The Venetians cook with white polenta (thinner and lighter than slow-cook versions from outside the area) and traditionally serve it with braises. This recipe uses milk to give the same soft melting texture, more like semolina than the firmer, coarser polenta you find further south in Italy.

500ml water
375ml milk
1 teaspoon salt
220g slow-cook polenta
45g butter
3 tablespoons freshly grated parmesan cheese
squeeze lemon juice

Place the water, milk and salt in a saucepan and bring to a simmer over medium heat. Slowly pour in the polenta, whisking continuously. Continue to cook, stirring often, for about 45 minutes. Remove the pan from the heat and beat in the butter, parmesan and lemon juice. Check the seasoning before serving, adding more salt if needed. **SERVES 4**

RIGATONI AND UMBRIAN SAUSAGE RAGU

2 tablespoons olive oil
6 good-quality coarse pork sausages
1 onion, sliced
1 carrot, sliced
2 celery sticks, sliced
2 garlic cloves, sliced
400g tin diced tomatoes
375ml chicken stock
1 bay leaf
½ teaspoon sugar
400g paccheri rigati or rigatoni
freshly grated pecorino romano cheese, to serve
handful basil leaves, to serve

Heat the oil in a large heavy-based frying pan over medium heat. Squeeze the sausage meat out of the skins into the pan, breaking it into chunky pieces, and fry for 10 minutes, until golden. Add the onion, carrot and celery and cook for a further 10 minutes, until very soft and starting to colour.

Add the garlic and cook for a further minute, then stir in the tomatoes, stock and bay leaf. Increase the heat to bring to the boil then lower the heat and simmer gently for 45–50 minutes, until the sauce is thick. Add the sugar and season with sea salt and freshly ground black pepper. Remove from the heat.

Cook the pasta in a large saucepan of boiling salted water according to the instructions on the packet, until al dente. Drain well. Return to the pan and stir through the ragu. Serve immediately with the grated pecorino and basil. SERVES 4

PAPPARDELLE AND SPICY CHICKEN RAGU

2 tablespoons olive oil
8 chicken thighs, skin on
220g pancetta, diced
1 onion, sliced
1 carrot, sliced
2 celery sticks, sliced
2 bay leaves
2 rosemary sprigs
2 garlic cloves, sliced
2 teaspoons dried chilli flakes
125ml dry white wine
375ml chicken stock
400g pappardelle
knob of butter
freshly grated parmesan cheese, to serve

Heat a little of the oil in a wide, shallow casserole dish over medium–high heat. Season the chicken with sea salt and freshly ground black pepper and fry, skin side down, for about 10 minutes, until the skin is golden and crisp. If necessary, do this in batches. Remove from the dish and set aside. Add the pancetta and cook until golden, then remove and set aside with the chicken.

Heat the remaining oil and stir in the onion, carrot, celery, bay leaves and rosemary. Cook for 10 minutes, or until the vegetables are really soft, then add the garlic and chilli flakes and cook for a further minute. Increase the heat, tip in the wine and boil for 2 minutes to cook off the alcohol. Return the chicken and pancetta, pour in the stock and cook for 45 minutes–1 hour, until the sauce is reduced and the chicken is very tender.

Remove the chicken with a slotted spoon and leave to cool for a few minutes, then shred the meat from the bones using a fork. Stir the meat into the sauce and discard the skin and bones. Add sea salt and freshly ground pepper to taste.

Cook the pasta in a large saucepan of boiling salted water until al dente, according to the instructions on the packet, and drain well. Return to the pan with a knob of butter and toss through the ragu. Serve with the grated parmesan. SERVES 4

These are variations on a classic Umbrian ragu. While I was testing the recipes, my Italian friend tried them out on her family, who were shocked to discover chicken in the ragu. Thankfully, the chook did me proud and was awarded the 'Italian nonna seal of approval'.

OK, meat loaf isn't the most glamorous of dishes (you'll notice our talented art director has left it in the distance of a beautiful street shot). But life isn't all about looks and meat loaf always tastes great, plus the leftovers make a delicious (although perhaps not pretty) sandwich filling the next day. This Italian version has pancetta, ricotta and parsley.

BELLISSIMO MEAT LOAF

1 tablespoon olive oil, plus extra for greasing
1 onion, finely chopped
185g pancetta, finely chopped
2 garlic cloves, chopped
1kg beef mince
45g fresh breadcrumbs
3 tablespoons freshly grated parmesan cheese
handful flat-leaf parsley, chopped
1 egg, lightly beaten
125g ricotta cheese
simple tomato salad (see recipe)

Preheat the oven to 180°C/gas mark 4. Grease a 900g/2lb loaf tin with plenty of oil. Heat the oil in a large non-stick frying pan over medium heat, add the onion and pancetta and cook for 6–8 minutes, until the pancetta is crisp. Add the garlic and stir for 1 minute. Remove from the heat and allow to cool.

Place the beef in a large bowl and add the breadcrumbs, parmesan, parsley and plenty of sea salt and freshly ground black pepper. Tip in the cooled onion and pancetta and the egg, and mix well with your hands to combine. Gently work through the ricotta, not doing too thorough a job of it. Pack into the loaf tin, pressing down lightly to fit in all the mixture. Bake for 50–60 minutes, until the top is golden brown and the loaf is coming away from the sides of the tin. Remove from the oven and allow to cool for about 10 minutes before slicing and serving with the tomato salad. SERVES 6

SIMPLE TOMATO SALAD

500g ripe salad tomatoes, sliced
2 tablespoons extra-virgin olive oil
2 teaspoons red wine vinegar
½ teaspoon dried oregano

Lay the tomato slices on a large plate. Combine the oil, vinegar and oregano in a bowl and spoon over the tomatoes. Season with sea salt and set aside for 30 minutes to allow the flavours to mingle.
SERVES 4–6

BAKED CABBAGE AND BREAD SOUP

This hearty peasant dish originated on the island of Sardinia. Its crisp golden topping and layers of toasted bread make it more like a gratinated stew than a soup. Stew or soup, it makes a perfect supper for a cold winter evening.

500g crusty bread, cut into 1cm slices
4 garlic cloves, 1 peeled and whole,
　3 thinly sliced
4 tablespoons olive oil, plus extra to drizzle
1 onion, thinly sliced
1kg savoy cabbage, core removed
　and leaves shredded
8 anchovy fillets in olive oil, drained and chopped
3 tablespoons coarsely grated parmesan cheese,
　plus extra to serve
¼ teaspoon freshly grated nutmeg
1.25 litres chicken stock

Preheat the oven to 200°C/gas mark 6. Lay the slices of bread on two large baking sheets and toast in the oven for 10 minutes, until lightly golden and a little crisp but not dry. Rub all over with the whole garlic clove and set aside.

Heat the oil in a large frying pan over medium–high heat. Add the sliced garlic and cook for a few seconds, until fragrant. Add the onion and cabbage and stir the anchovy through until melted into the mix. Remove from the heat.

Line one-third of the toasts in the base of a round, heavy-based ovenproof dish, about 8cm deep x 23cm wide, breaking the bread slices to fit the dish if you need to. Pile on half the cabbage mix and top with one-third of the cheese and a grating of nutmeg. Repeat this layering once more and finish with a layer of toast. Pour over the stock and submerge the bread lightly with the back of a spoon. Sprinkle over the remaining parmesan and a final grating of nutmeg. Place in the oven and bake for 25–30 minutes. The soup will be golden and crisp on top. Serve a spoonful of the soft soup with some crispy topping and extra parmesan.

SERVES 4

LIGURIAN FISH STEW

2 tablespoons olive oil, plus extra to serve
1 onion, sliced
1 fennel bulb, cut into thin wedges,
   fronds chopped
2 garlic cloves, sliced
300ml dry white wine
400g tin cherry tomatoes
1.25 litres fish stock
500g new potatoes, peeled
500g firm white fish fillets, such as monkfish,
   cod or haddock, cut into 4cm chunks
3 small sardines, gutted
350g small squid, cleaned and cut into chunks
6 langoustines or large raw prawns in their shells
500g mussels, cleaned
handful flat-leaf parsley, to serve

Heat the oil in a large heavy-based saucepan over
low heat. Add the onion and fennel wedges and
cook, stirring occasionally, for 8 minutes, to soften.
Add the garlic and cook for 1 minute. Increase the
heat to high, pour in the wine and boil for 1 minute.
Add the tomatoes and cook for 5 minutes. Add the
stock and potatoes and bring to the boil, then lower
the heat to a gentle simmer. Cook for 20 minutes,
or until the potatoes are almost tender.

Add the white fish and sardines and simmer gently
for 3 minutes. Stir in the squid, langoustines or
prawns and the mussels. After about 6 minutes,
or once the mussels have opened, remove the pan
from the heat and set aside for 5 minutes. Serve
with a scattering of parsley and fennel fronds and
a drizzle of olive oil. SERVES 4-6

THREE MUSHROOM AND BARLEY SOUP

30g dried porcini mushrooms
2 tablespoons olive oil
250g fresh porcini mushrooms, sliced
100g chanterelles
2 garlic cloves, chopped
1 tablespoon thyme leaves
150g pearl barley
2 litres vegetable or chicken stock
handful flat-leaf parsley, chopped
extra-virgin olive oil, to serve

Soak the dried porcini in 50ml warm water for 30 minutes, until soft. Drain the porcini, reserving the liquid, and chop. Set aside.

Heat the olive oil in a large, heavy-based saucepan over high heat. Add the fresh mushrooms, season with sea salt and freshly ground black pepper and fry for 1–2 minutes, until golden. Add the garlic and thyme and fry for a further minute. Remove the mushrooms and garlic and set aside.

Stir the pearl barley into the pan and add the stock, scraping the bottom of the pan to collect up the flavours. Strain the porcini soaking liquid into the pan and add the chopped porcini. Cook for 40–45 minutes, until the barley is tender.

Return the mushrooms and garlic to the pan and cook for a few minutes to heat through. To serve, ladle the soup into four bowls, scatter with parsley and drizzle with extra-virgin olive oil. **SERVES 4**

Short ribs are becoming ever more popular, and for good reason: the meat cooks slowly on the bone until meltingly tender; they're better value than cubes of lean meat; and they're much more fun to pick up with sticky fingers. Use them for any slow-cooked dish, even curry.

SPICY BEEF SHORT RIBS

1 tablespoon olive oil
2kg beef short ribs
2 carrots, sliced
1 onion, sliced
2 celery sticks, sliced
2 garlic cloves, sliced
2 red chillies, chopped
2 rosemary sprigs
2 x 400g tins diced tomatoes
4 tablespoons soft brown sugar
3 tablespoons balsamic vinegar
500ml beef stock

Preheat the oven to 160°C/gas mark 3. Heat the oil in a large roasting tin over medium–high heat. Season the ribs with sea salt and freshly ground black pepper and fry them, turning regularly, until browned all over. You may have to do this in batches. Stir in the carrot, onion, celery, garlic and chilli and cook for 2–3 minutes longer, until the vegetables start to brown. Add the rosemary, tomatoes, sugar, vinegar and stock and mix well to combine. Bring to the boil, then transfer to the oven and cook, uncovered, for 2–2½ hours, or until the sauce has thickened and the meat is falling off the bones. Remove from the oven and allow to stand for a few minutes. Check the seasoning before serving. SERVES 4-6

CELERIAC AND RADICCHIO GRATIN

This is a wonderful alternative to a classic potato gratin. The radicchio has a delicious bitterness that keeps the cream and cheese in their place.

300ml double cream
125ml milk
2 garlic cloves, sliced
2 rosemary sprigs, leaves picked and chopped
1kg celeriac, thinly sliced
½ head radicchio, leaves torn
80g parmesan cheese, freshly grated

Preheat the oven to 180°C/gas mark 4. Put the cream, milk, garlic, rosemary and celeriac into a saucepan over low heat and slowly bring to the boil. Remove from the heat and spoon half the mixture into a 30cm round ovenproof dish. Top with half the radicchio and half the parmesan, then pour in the remaining celeriac and cover with the remaining radicchio and parmesan. Bake for 30–35 minutes, or until the celeriac is tender and the surface is golden and bubbling. SERVES 4

PROSCIUTTO AND FONTINA CRESPELLE BAKE

30g butter, plus extra for greasing
3 endives, each cut into 4 long wedges
12 slices prosciutto
80ml milk
3 tablespoons dry white wine
200g fontina cheese, chopped
4 tablespoons freshly grated parmesan cheese
for the crespelle
150g plain flour
250ml milk
15g butter, melted
2 eggs, lightly beaten

To make the crespelle, beat the flour, milk, melted butter and egg in a jug and allow to stand for 30 minutes. Heat a non-stick frying pan over medium–high heat. Rub the pan with a little butter, pour in a couple of tablespoons of batter and swirl the pan to coat the base. Cook for 2–3 minutes, then flip and cook the other side for 1 minute. Slide onto a plate and continue making the crespelle until all the batter is used.

Preheat the oven to 200°C/gas mark 6. Melt the butter in a large frying pan over medium heat, until sizzling. Add the endive and fry for 2–3 minutes on each side, until golden brown. Set aside for a few minutes until cool enough to handle. Wrap each wedge in a slice of prosciutto, then half a crespelle.

To assemble the bake, combine the milk and wine and pour them into the base of a medium-sized ovenproof dish. Lay the wrapped endives in the dish, dot over the fontina and top with the parmesan. Bake for 25–30 minutes, until golden and bubbling, and serve. SERVES 4

AUBERGINE PARMIGIANA

For parmigiana the aubergine is traditionally fried,
which does give it a certain silkiness. I prefer to
grill mine, leaving it with a touch of bite, as I find
the cheese makes this dish rich enough.

3 large aubergines, cut into 1cm rounds
2 tablespoons olive oil
220g fontina cheese, sliced
3 tablespoons freshly grated parmesan cheese
85g ricotta cheese, crumbled
handful basil leaves
for the tomato sauce
600g tinned diced tomatoes
2 garlic cloves, crushed
1 tablespoon olive oil

To make the tomato sauce, simmer the tomatoes
in a saucepan for 2 minutes. Remove from the heat
and stir in the garlic and olive oil. Season with sea
salt and set aside.

Heat the grill to medium. Place the aubergine onto
lightly greased baking trays, drizzle with the olive
oil and sprinkle with sea salt and freshly ground
black pepper. Grill for 2–3 minutes on each side,
or until golden and softening. Loosely cover with
cling film and leave to cool on the trays. Preheat
the oven to 200°C/gas mark 6.

To assemble the parmigiana, ladle a spoonful of
the tomato sauce into the base of a 30cm round
ovenproof dish. Layer one-third of the aubergine
on top, add half the fontina and a light covering of
parmesan. Repeat. Top with the remaining tomato
sauce and aubergine, and finish with the ricotta,
basil and a generous sprinkling of parmesan. Cover
with foil and bake for 20 minutes, then remove
the foil and bake for a further 30 minutes, or until
golden and bubbling. Leave to stand for a few
minutes before serving. SERVES 4

For a main course it's nice to make meatballs larger and serve just one per person. The sultanas keep them moist and the pine nuts and marjoram let you know you're eating Italian. The tomato sauce is made with tinned diced tomatoes. I recently learnt something interesting from an Italian tomato farmer: the ripest, most flavoursome tomatoes are used in these tins because they're easier to chop than the ones that end up tinned whole.

BRAISED PORK MEATBALLS

1kg pork mince
25g sultanas, roughly chopped
45g toasted pine nuts, roughly chopped
2 tablespoons freshly grated parmesan cheese,
    plus extra to serve
1 tablespoon roughly chopped marjoram
freshly grated nutmeg
grated zest 1 lemon
45g fresh white breadcrumbs
1 egg white, lightly beaten
2 tablespoons olive oil
430ml chicken stock
2 x 400g tins diced tomatoes
250g cherry tomatoes
2 bay leaves
squeeze lemon juice
steamed snake or green beans
    dressed in olive oil, to serve

Put the mince in a large bowl with the sultanas, pine nuts, grated parmesan and the marjoram. Add a good grating of fresh nutmeg, the lemon zest, breadcrumbs, sea salt and freshly ground black pepper, and use your hands to combine. Tip in the egg white and continue squeezing the ingredients together until well combined. Wet your hands to break up and roll the mixture into large meatballs, then place them in the fridge to chill for 30 minutes.

Heat the oil in a large, non-stick heavy-based frying pan over medium–high heat. Fry the meatballs, turning frequently, until golden brown. Remove from the pan once they have a nice colour. You might have to do this in batches.

Increase the heat, pour in the stock and let bubble for a few minutes, scraping the bottom of the pan with a wooden spoon to collect up the flavours. Return the meatballs to the pan with the tinned and cherry tomatoes and bay leaves. Reduce the heat, cover with a tight-fitting lid and simmer for 20–25 minutes, until the meatballs are cooked through. Remove from the heat and add a squeeze of lemon juice. Serve topped with the extra parmesan and green beans on the side. SERVES 4-6

When I was a bright young thing, I loved eating out at the latest special restaurants. I don't dine out so much these days (the music's too loud and I'm starting to have to squint to read the menu). Now I invite friends to my home and cook for them. If that sounds like hard work, let me stress that I believe eating dinner with friends should be a joy, never a chore. That's the cornerstone of the following five menus. (See how I've taken on board the Italian way of doing things?) Nothing is overly complicated or fussy here, it's simply that the ingredients are a bit more luxurious than for a usual weekday dinner. I might even cook a couple of these for the family – on a good night, if they've been very well-behaved!

con amici

DINNER

BRAISED BROAD BEANS AND PANCETTA ON TOAST

2 tablespoons olive oil, plus extra to drizzle
200g pancetta, cut into lardons
2 shallots, finely chopped
2 garlic cloves, 1 chopped, 1 whole
375g broad beans (podded weight)
125ml chicken stock
1 tablespoon chopped mint leaves
squeeze lemon juice
4 large slices chunky bread
parmesan cheese shavings, to serve

Heat the oil in a large frying pan over medium heat, add the pancetta and cook until well browned. Tip in the shallot and chopped garlic and cook for a further 2 minutes, stirring frequently, until the shallot is starting to soften. Add the beans and stir to coat. Pour in the stock, bring to the boil and cover and simmer for 6–8 minutes, until the beans are really tender and the sauce has thickened. Stir in the mint and cook for 1 minute. Remove from the heat and season with sea salt and freshly ground black pepper and a squeeze of lemon juice.

Heat the griddle to hot, toast the bread on each side until crisp and golden, and rub with the garlic clove. Serve with the broad beans and pancetta scattered with parmesan and a drizzle of olive oil.
SERVES 4

SEA BASS, CLAM AND FENNEL BROTH

The flavours here are delicate and the success of the broth hangs on the quality of the seafood and stock you use. Buy good-quality fish stock or make your own, using bones and offcuts from your fishmonger. Chop an onion, carrot and celery stick and gently fry in olive oil for 5 minutes. Add 500g fish offcuts, 1 tablespoon white wine vinegar, 1 teaspoon salt and 1 litre water. Simmer for 30 minutes, then strain the stock before using.

2 tablespoons olive oil, plus extra to serve
1 fennel bulb, cut into thin wedges,
   fronds reserved
2 bay leaves
1 garlic clove, crushed
½ teaspoon dried chilli flakes
500g sea bass fillets, skin on, cut into 5cm pieces
500g clams, cleaned
430ml fish stock, heated
handful flat-leaf parsley, to serve

Heat the oil in a large deep-sided pan with a lid. Add the fennel wedges and bay leaves and sweat for about 10 minutes, or until the fennel is soft but not coloured. Add the garlic and chilli flakes and cook for a further minute. Season the fish with sea salt and add it to the pan, skin side up. Cover and cook for 3 minutes. Tip in the clams, being careful not to break up the fish. Pour in the hot stock and cover and cook for another 3 minutes, or until the clams have opened. Discard any that remain closed. Stir through the fennel fronds with the parsley and drizzle with olive oil to serve. **SERVES 4**

Menu Uno

Once upon a time, when my life was a lot less interesting, I used to double skin my broad beans. My position on this has become clearer as I've got older – if you've got time to shell beans, get a hobby!

GRIDDLED SQUID, HERB SALAD AND BLACK OLIVE DRESSING

600g cleaned squid, scored on the inside
  and cut into thick strips
1 tablespoon olive oil
½ teaspoon dried chilli flakes
small bunch flat-leaf parsley, leaves picked
small bunch basil, leaves picked
small bunch mint, leaves picked
lemon wedges, to serve
for the dressing
30g pitted black olives, torn
2 shallots, thinly sliced
juice 1 lemon
4 tablespoons olive oil
1 garlic clove, crushed
½ red chilli, sliced

To make the dressing, mix the olives, shallots, lemon juice and olive oil in a bowl with the garlic, chilli and a pinch of sea salt. Set aside.

Pat the squid dry with kitchen paper and toss with the olive oil and chilli flakes. Preheat a barbecue or a chargrill pan on high heat. Cook the squid for 1 minute on each side, until just cooked. Set aside.

Spread the herbs on a big platter, scatter over the squid and spoon over the dressing. Serve with the lemon wedges. **SERVES 4**

menu due This is all about the grilling, so it's a great menu for anyone wanting to display a touch of Italian machismo. (It's the sort of dinner I might make, with lots of subconscious crashing of cast iron and hissing of gas flames, after I've had to bake 25 pink cupcakes for a tweenage girl's birthday party.)

ROAST RIB-EYE

2 rosemary sprigs, roughly chopped
1 tablespoon thyme leaves
1 tablespoon olive oil
2 x 2-bone rib-eye steaks on the bone
   (about 400g each)
lemon braised potatoes and artichokes
   (see recipe), to serve

Preheat the oven to 200°C/gas mark 6. Combine
the rosemary, thyme and olive oil in a bowl and rub
all over the steaks, then season with sea salt and
freshly ground black pepper.

Heat a large griddle pan or heavy-based frying pan
over high heat to smoking hot. Add the steaks
and cook for 2–3 minutes on each side, until well
browned. Transfer the pan to the oven and roast
for 8 minutes for medium–rare, longer if you prefer
your beef more cooked through. Remove from the
oven and allow to rest for 5 minutes.

Carve the steaks on a board and serve with lemon
braised potatoes and artichokes. SERVES 4

LEMON BRAISED POTATOES AND ARTICHOKES

2 tablespoons olive oil
200g good-quality artichokes in olive oil,
   plus 2 tablespoons of their oil
3 shallots, thinly sliced
2 garlic cloves, finely chopped
1 bay leaf
500g medium waxy potatoes,
   peeled and quartered
½ lemon, cut into four

Pour the olive oil and the reserved artichoke oil into
a large heavy-based pan just big enough to hold the
vegetables in one layer and heat over medium heat.
Add the shallots and cook for 6–7 minutes, until
softened and translucent. Add the garlic and bay
leaf, cook for 1 minute, then toss in the potatoes
and lemon pieces. Season with sea salt and freshly
ground black pepper.

Pour in enough water to come one-quarter of the
way up the potatoes. Increase the heat and bring
to the boil, then lower to a slow simmer. Cover
with a tight-fitting lid and cook for 10 minutes,
or until the potatoes feel tender when pierced
with a fork. Add the artichokes, increase the heat
and cook, uncovered, for 5 minutes, until heated
through and most of the liquid has been absorbed.
SERVES 4

PEAS, SPINACH AND TORN MOZZARELLA

2 garlic cloves, unpeeled and bashed
500g fresh peas (podded weight)
handful baby spinach leaves
handful mint leaves
handful basil leaves
handful flat-leaf parsley
3 tablespoons olive oil
juice ½ small orange
juice ½ lemon
2 x125g balls mozzarella cheese, torn
¼ teaspoon dried chilli flakes
toasted bread, to serve

Put the garlic in a large pan of salted water and
bring to the boil. Add the peas and cook for about
3 minutes, until just soft. Drain, discard the garlic
and toss the peas into a bowl with the baby spinach,
herbs, olive oil, and orange and lemon juice. Season
with sea salt and freshly ground black pepper and
top with the mozzarella. Sprinkle with the chilli
flakes and serve with toasted bread. SERVES 4

MONKFISH, RED PEPPER, POTATO AND TOMATO ROAST

500g new potatoes, halved
2 red peppers, deseeded and cut into thick strips
3 garlic cloves, unpeeled and bashed
3 rosemary sprigs
4 anchovy fillets, roughly chopped
2 tablespoons olive oil
500g cherry tomatoes, halved
500g firm white fish fillets, such as monkfish,
   cod or haddock, cut into 5cm chunks
handful flat-leaf parsley, to serve
2 tablespoons capers, drained

Preheat the oven to 200°C/gas mark 6. Place the
potatoes, peppers, garlic and rosemary in a large
baking tray. Scatter over the anchovy fillets, drizzle
with the oil and roast for 40 minutes, until the
potatoes are starting to soften and turn golden.
Remove the tray from the oven, stir in the tomatoes
and roast for a further 10 minutes.

Season the fish with sea salt and freshly ground
black pepper. Place it over the vegetables and
roast for a final 10 minutes, or until the fish is just
cooked through. Scatter with parsley and capers
before serving. SERVES 4

menu tre

I always feel very at home in Italy. The sun, the light, the warmth,
the olive trees and the big sky remind me of Australia. Although,
I suspect it's actually the relaxed way of life, even in the most
bustling of cities, that makes us all want to be a 'little bit Italian'.

SHAVED CABBAGE, FINOCCHIONA, PARMESAN AND HAZELNUTS

juice 1 lemon
2 tablespoons extra-virgin olive oil
pinch caster sugar
½ savoy cabbage
10 slices finocchiona, torn
2 heads radicchio, leaves separated
handful basil leaves
30g parmesan cheese, shaved
90g roasted hazelnuts, roughly crushed

Mix together the lemon juice, olive oil and sugar in a bowl and season with sea salt and freshly ground black pepper. Shred the cabbage and toss in the dressing. Leave to stand for 10 minutes.

Divide the shredded cabbage between six plates, drape the finocchiona beside it and top with the radicchio, basil and parmesan. Scatter with the hazelnuts and serve. **SERVES 6**

menu quattro Salami, coppa, pancetta, prosciutto ... The Italian way with pig is world famous, and there's a definite pork theme running through this menu. The cabbage salad is served as the starter, with the finocchiona (Tuscan fennel salami) linking its flavours to the roast pork and the pancetta in the lentils.

ROAST PORK WITH BAY AND VINEGAR

Mostarda di Cremona tastes like a bitey-sweet cross between mustard and mango chutney. It's traditionally served at New Year with ham and sausages and will last for ages in the fridge. The onions tossed in the syrupy balsamic glaze take on a fantastic flavour – like a sweet and sour onion jam. You don't need expensive aged balsamic vinegar here, as it's going in the roasting tin.

4 garlic cloves, unpeeled and bashed
2 red onions, cut into wedges
10 bay leaves
2kg pork loin, chined and skin scored
  (ask your butcher to do this)
1 tablespoon olive oil
2 teaspoons dried chilli flakes
1 teaspoon sea salt
1 tablespoon light soft brown sugar
125ml balsamic vinegar
lentils and pancetta (see recipe), to serve
mostarda di Cremona, to serve

Preheat the oven to 220°C/gas mark 7. Put the garlic, onion wedges and bay leaves in a roasting tin and place the loin on top, making sure it covers all the vegetables. Mix the oil, chilli flakes and salt together in a bowl and rub over the pork and into the scored skin. Roast for 30 minutes, then reduce the heat to 180°C/gas mark 4 and roast for 1 hour.

Remove the tin from the oven and spoon out any fat. Stir the sugar into the vinegar until dissolved, then pour it over the pork. Return the tin to the oven and roast for a further 30 minutes.

Place the pork on a carving board, cover it loosely with foil and let it rest for 15 minutes before serving. Discard the bay leaves from the roasting tin and squeeze the garlic flesh out of its skin. Stir the garlic and onions through the balsamic juices and keep warm until ready to serve.

Carve the pork into slices and serve with the onions, lentils and pancetta, and mostarda on the side.
SERVES 6

LENTILS AND PANCETTA

1 tablespoon olive oil, plus extra to drizzle
200g pancetta, diced
1 large carrot, sliced
1 celery stick, sliced
1 onion, finely chopped
1 red chilli, finely chopped
2 garlic cloves, crushed
2 rosemary sprigs, finely chopped
200g Castelluccio or Puy lentils
500ml chicken stock

Heat the olive oil in a large, heavy-based frying pan. Add the pancetta and cook until starting to crisp and turn golden. Remove with a slotted spoon and set aside.

Reduce the heat to low. Add the carrot, celery and onion and cook for 10 minutes, until the vegetables are really soft. Add the chilli, garlic and rosemary and cook for a further 2 minutes. Stir in the pancetta and the lentils. Pour in the stock and bring to the boil, then reduce the heat and simmer for 25 minutes, until the lentils are just tender. Drizzle with olive oil and serve. **SERVES 6**

This is my 'celebration of pork' menu. I've noticed the Italians often

serve a cold starter, even before a roast during the winter months.

BRESAOLA, BEETROOT, RICOTTA AND ROCKET SALAD

I love the idea of carpaccio but I think it's almost impossible to do well at home – this is a cheat's easy version. Bresaola is air-dried salted beef from northern Italy and makes a perfect alternative to wafer-thin sliced raw fillet.

3 tablespoons olive oil
1 tablespoon green peppercorns
1 shallot, finely sliced
juice ½ lemon
2 cooked beetroots, cut into large chunks
large handful wild rocket
16 slices bresaola
250g ricotta cheese

Mix the olive oil, peppercorns, shallot and lemon juice in a bowl with sea salt and freshly ground black pepper. Toss in the beetroot and rocket.

Divide the bresaola between four plates. Add a pile of beetroot and leaves, break the ricotta over the top and spoon over any extra dressing to finish.
SERVES 4

ROASTED POUSSINS WITH WALNUT AND CHERRY STUFFING

4 poussins
12 thin slices pancetta
1 tablespoon olive oil
<u>for the stuffing</u>
40g butter
1 onion, finely chopped
2 garlic cloves, crushed
150g walnuts, chopped
150g crusty bread, torn into bite-sized chunks
45g dried cherries, chopped
2 tablespoons thyme leaves
grated zest ½ lemon
3 tablespoons olive oil
1 teaspoon dried chilli flakes

To make the stuffing, melt the butter in a large non-stick frying pan until sizzling. Add the onion and cook, stirring occasionally, for 6–8 minutes, until softened. Add the garlic and cook for a further minute. Tip into a bowl and toss through the remaining ingredients to combine.

Preheat the oven to 180°C/gas mark 4. Spoon stuffing into each poussin, not packing them too tightly, and tie the legs together with string. Set the remaining stuffing aside. Drape the pancetta over the poussins and transfer to a roasting tin. Drizzle with the oil and roast for 20 minutes. Place the reserved stuffing in the tin, nestled around the poussins, and roast for a further 15 minutes.

Remove from the oven, cover loosely with foil to keep warm and leave to rest for 10 minutes. Serve scattered with the extra stuffing. **SERVES 4**

menu cinque

Poussin with walnut and cherry stuffing sounds sophisticated but
it's one of the least tricky dinner party dishes you'll come across.
You can even make the easy stuffing and fill the birds in advance.

We were in the house for less than an hour before Anna-Maria, our Italian 'holiday neighbour', appeared at the window with wine and limoncello, lemons and herbs. She introduced us to her daughter (the town parking officer, and a most useful friend to have) and within a day we had an instant Italian family. Within three more days we were getting used to the idea that up to fifteen of our new family could drop in at any time – even breakfast – for an impromptu party (something likely to give me a heart attack if it ever happened at home). They arrived in loud laughing groups, with presents from their gardens and plates to share. Their spontaneous celebrations of life needed nothing more than a group of happy people wanting to eat together and a big enough table to put the platters on.

POTATO, PORCINI AND MOZZARELLA CROCCHETTE

800g floury potatoes
30g dried porcini mushrooms
125g ball mozzarella cheese, roughly chopped
115g plain flour
3 eggs, lightly beaten
150g white breadcrumbs
1 litre light-flavoured oil, for deep frying

Preheat the oven to 200°C/gas mark 6. Pierce the potatoes all over with a fork. Place directly on the top shelf of the oven and bake for 1 hour, or until tender. Meanwhile, soak the porcini in boiling water until soft. Drain and set aside.

Remove the potatoes from the oven and set aside until cool enough to handle. Halve the potatoes and scoop the centre into a bowl. Mash with some sea salt and freshly ground black pepper. Roughly chop the mushrooms and stir into the potato with the mozzarella. Form the mixture into 16 sausage shapes. Place on a tray and chill for 30 minutes.

Put the flour on a plate with some seasoning, the beaten egg in a shallow bowl and the breadcrumbs in a baking tray. Dust the crocchette in flour, dip in the egg then roll in the breadcrumbs. Chill for a further 30 minutes, or overnight.

Heat the oil in a large deep-sided pan to 180°C, or until a piece of bread fries golden in 20 seconds. Fry the crocchette in batches for 3–4 minutes, until golden, turning them occasionally so they cook evenly. Drain on kitchen paper and sprinkle with a little salt before serving. MAKES 16

These antipasti can be served as starters, or become an entire meal in themselves. In Italy, my children often ate these crocchette with a bit of salad for dinner. And who can blame them? What's not to love about fried mashed potato?

MARJORAM AND CHILLI GRILLED VEGETABLES

The vinegar here sharpens the flavours and gives this a slightly Greek rather than Italian flavour (shhhh). It's inspired by my mum, who, in the seventies, embraced grilled, stuffed and marinated vegetables with great fervour.

4 tablespoons olive oil
2 aubergines, cut lengthways into 1cm thick slices
2 courgettes, cut lengthways into 0.5cm thick slices
2 red peppers, deseeded and quartered
2 yellow peppers, deseeded and quartered
for the dressing
1 tablespoon finely chopped marjoram
2 garlic cloves, finely chopped
1 red chilli, deseeded and finely chopped
2 tablespoons olive oil
1 tablespoon red wine vinegar

Preheat a barbecue or griddle pan to hot. Brush the vegetables with a little olive oil. Cook the aubergine slices for 1–2 minutes on each side. Transfer to a large plate, drizzle with a little more oil and cover loosely with cling film. Set aside. Cook the courgettes for 1 minute on each side, remove and add to the aubergine. Cook the peppers for 2–3 minutes, turning until charred and softened. Remove and add to the aubergine and courgette, drizzle with a little more oil and some sea salt and freshly ground black pepper. Allow to cool.

To make the dressing, combine the marjoram, garlic and chilli with the olive oil and red wine vinegar, stirring well.

Lay the antipasto on a platter and spoon over the dressing. You can eat immediately, but if you leave the vegetables to marinate for at least 30 minutes, they'll taste even better.

SERVES 6–8 AS PART OF AN ANTIPASTO PLATTER

GREEN OLIVES, ORANGE AND FENNEL SEEDS

1 teaspoon fennel seeds
2 tablespoons extra-virgin olive oil
1 orange
375g pitted large green olives

Toast the fennel seeds in a frying pan over low heat, shaking the pan until they release their aroma. Tip into a mortar and pestle and grind to a coarse powder. Transfer to a bowl with the olive oil and season lightly with sea salt.

Segment the orange and cut the flesh into small pieces. Stuff a piece into each of the olives and transfer to a bowl, also adding any remaining orange pieces. Toss to combine and leave to marinate for at least 30 minutes.

SERVES 6–8 AS PART OF AN ANTIPASTO PLATTER

THYME AND CHILLI BAKED RICOTTA

2 x 250g ricotta cheeses
3 garlic cloves, thinly sliced
2 thyme sprigs
1 teaspoon dried chilli flakes
2 tablespoons olive oil
grilled crusty bread, to serve

Preheat the oven to 200°C/gas mark 6. Take 4 30cm square pieces of parchment paper and lay 2 pieces on top of each other at different angles. Put 1 ricotta in the centre of each double layer. Divide the garlic, thyme and chilli flakes and add to each parcel with a drizzle of olive oil. Gather the paper to form 2 parcels and secure with string. Put on a baking tray and cook for 20 minutes, taking care the paper doesn't come into contact with the top of the oven.

Remove from the oven, untie the parcels and drizzle with olive oil. Spread on toasts.

SERVES 6–8 AS PART OF AN ANTIPASTO PLATTER

MIXED MEAT GRILL

2 tablespoons olive oil
2 garlic cloves, crushed
500g pork loin, cut into 2cm cubes
1 lemon, cut into chunks
12 sage leaves
8 lamb cutlets
12 coarse pork sausages
spicy salsa rossa (see recipe), to serve
pistachio and chilli pesto (see page 39), to serve
lemon wedges, to serve

Mix together the olive oil and garlic. Set aside.
Thread the diced pork onto skewers with chunks
of lemon and sage leaves to make kebabs. Brush
the kebabs and lamb cutlets with the garlic oil
and set aside. Heat a griddle or barbecue to hot.

Cook the kebabs for 10–12 minutes, turning until
browned all over. Cook the sausages, turning
frequently, for 15–20 minutes, until cooked through.
Cook the lamb cutlets for 2–3 minutes on each side.

Place all the meat on a big platter and serve with
the salsa, pesto and lemon wedges. SERVES 6–8

SPICY SALSA ROSSA

2 garlic cloves, crushed
1 red onion, thinly sliced
1 red chilli, finely chopped
4 anchovy fillets, finely chopped
3 tablespoons olive oil
2 tablespoons red wine vinegar
4 roasted red peppers in olive oil,
   drained and chopped
4 plum tomatoes, seeded and chopped

Mix all the ingredients together in a bowl with
some sea salt and freshly ground black pepper.
Set aside until ready to use.

After years of research, I've decided by far the easiest and most fun summer party food is an outdoor grill with a few different salads (a lot of man-hours in Australia have been devoted to this important study). Friends can keep you company while you're cooking (most guys can't resist the primeval lure of fire, meat and barbecue tongs). Put your energy into making great salsas and pesto to go with the grill; choose a couple of salads and do them well. Serve everything together and then sit down and enjoy the company.

POTATO SALAD (AGAIN)

As regular readers have perhaps noticed, I can never get enough of potato salad. I manage to shamelessly sneak a recipe into almost every book, and here it is again – perfect for serving with an Italian grill. I find traditional potato salad overpoweringly 'mayonnaisey' with rich meat and seafood, so I make my dressing half mayo, half yoghurt and add a squeeze of lemon for tang.

1kg baby salad potatoes, halved
1 fennel bulb, with fronds
1 long cucumber
1 tablespoon capers, drained
for the dressing
3 tablespoons mayonnaise
3 tablespoons plain yoghurt
squeeze lemon juice

To make the dressing, mix all the ingredients together in a bowl and season with sea salt and freshly ground black pepper. Set aside.

Cook the potatoes in salted boiling water for 12–15 minutes, until tender. Drain well and set aside to cool.

Cut the fennel into thin wedges and the cucumber into chunks. Combine them in a bowl with the fennel fronds, capers and cooled potatoes. Lightly toss in the dressing and serve.
SERVES 6–8, TOGETHER WITH OTHER SIDE DISHES

RAW GREEN VEGETABLES, SPELT, RICOTTA SALATA AND BITTER LEAF SALAD

When they're in season, you'll be able to find beautiful yellow courgette flowers to add to this.

100g spelt, rinsed
juice 1 lemon
4 tablespoons olive oil
1 fennel bulb
2 courgettes
200g asparagus, thinly sliced on the diagonal
small bunch basil, leaves picked
200g rocket leaves
100g ricotta salata, thinly sliced

Cook the spelt in salted boiling water for 20 minutes, until al dente. Drain. Toss in the lemon juice and olive oil and set aside to cool.

Use a mandolin or potato peeler to make thin fennel and courgette shavings. Toss into the cooled spelt, adding the asparagus, herbs and salad leaves. Season with sea salt and transfer to a large platter before topping with the ricotta salata.

SERVES 6–8, TOGETHER WITH OTHER SIDE DISHES

BEAN SALAD

3 tablespoons olive oil
1 red onion, thinly sliced
juice and zest 1 lemon
400g tin cannellini beans, rinsed and drained
250g broad beans (podded weight)
200g French beans, trimmed
2 slices rustic bread
½ garlic clove
60g parmesan cheese, shaved

Mix the olive oil, red onion and lemon zest and juice together in a bowl with sea salt and freshly ground black pepper. Toss in the cannellini.

Cook the broad beans in a pan of boiling salted water for 3 minutes. Tip in the French beans and continue to cook for 5 minutes, or until the beans are nice and tender. You want to go past the point of al dente with these. Drain. Tip into a big bowl, pour over the cannellini and dressing and allow to cool to room temperature.

Toast the bread until golden and beginning to char. Rub one side of each toast with garlic then chop into rough croutons. Toss through the beans with shaved parmesan, just before serving.

SERVES 6–8, TOGETHER WITH OTHER SIDE DISHES

A bean salad is an old classic and I had a hunch it was worth revisiting. So here it is: fresh, alive and delicious, and not at all embarrassed to be seen out partying in the 21st century.

MIXED FISH GRILL

1 octopus, cleaned
12 raw prawns in their shells
2 tablespoons olive oil
1 teaspoon dried chilli flakes
6 sardines, gutted
green olive and pine nut salsa
  (see recipe), to serve
roasted pepper and almond pesto
  (see page 39), to serve
lemon wedges, to serve

Place the octopus in a saucepan over high heat, tentacles facing downwards. Once you've heard it sizzle and release from the pan, pour in enough water to cover. Bring to the boil and simmer gently for 1 hour, or until the octopus is tender. Drain thoroughly, pat dry with kitchen paper and cut into 12 pieces.

Thread the prawns onto metal skewers. Mix together the olive oil and chilli flakes and brush the skewers, octopus and sardines. Season with salt.

Heat a griddle or barbecue to high. Cook the fish for 2–3 minutes on each side, until charred and cooked through. Place all the fish on a platter and serve with the salsa, pesto and lemon wedges.
SERVES 6–8

GREEN OLIVE AND PINE NUT SALSA

zest 2 lemons, juice of 1
3 tablespoons olive oil
125g pitted green olives, torn
1 small red onion, roughly chopped
1 garlic clove, crushed
50g toasted pine nuts
handful flat-leaf parsley, roughly chopped

Mix all the ingredients together in a bowl and set aside.

FRITTO MISTO PLATTER

3 artichokes
2 whole white fish, such as sea bass,
   sea bream or snapper, gutted
200g cleaned squid, cut into 2cm wide strips
6 raw prawns in their shells
6 langoustines
150g whitebait
3 small octopuses
115g plain flour
1 litre light-flavoured oil, for deep frying
1 lemon, cut into 1cm slices
1 orange, cut into 1cm slices
lemon wedges, to serve
orange wedges, to serve
good-quality bought mayonnaise, to serve

Preheat the oven to 150°C/gas mark 2 and line
a large baking tray with lots of kitchen paper.

Cut the stems off the artichokes, about 2cm from
the base. Pull away the outer leaves and discard,
stopping once the leaves start to look softer all the
way to the tip. Cut the artichokes in half and scoop
out the hairy chokes at the centre. Set aside. Cut
each whole fish into 3 pieces. Set aside.

Before you start frying, pat all the fish and seafood
with kitchen paper to remove any excess moisture.
Place the flour in a tray and season with sea salt
and freshly ground black pepper.

Heat the oil in a large deep-sided pan to 180°C, or
until a piece of bread fries golden in 20 seconds.
Toss the ingredients a few at a time in the seasoned
flour and fry in batches for 3–5 minutes, until
golden, starting with the artichokes and lemon and
orange slices so they don't take on the flavour of
the seafood. Remove with a slotted spoon, place
on the paper-lined tray and keep warm in the oven
while you cook all the fish and seafood in the same
way. Serve with the lemon and orange wedges
and lots of mayonnaise. SERVES 6–8

If you ever needed an excuse
to buy a deep-fryer, fritto
misto is it. One tip: if there's
an opportunity to deep-fry
outside, grab it. That way you
can serve your guests their
seafood crisp and hot from
the pan, and your house won't
smell like Harry Ramsden's
for a week afterwards.

BRAISED GREEN LEAVES

1kg savoy cabbage, cavolo nero,
   swiss chard or spinach
2 tablespoons olive oil
1 onion, thinly sliced
3 garlic cloves, sliced
1 teaspoon dried chilli flakes
2 rosemary sprigs, leaves picked and chopped
250ml chicken stock
15g butter
extra-virgin olive oil, to serve

Cut away the tough stalks of the cabbage and
slice the leaves thickly. Heat the olive oil in a large,
heavy-based saucepan over medium heat. Add
the onion and garlic and cook for 5 minutes, until
starting to soften but not colouring. Add the chilli
flakes and rosemary and cook for a further minute.
Add the cabbage leaves and stir to coat. Pour in the
stock and bring to the boil, then cover and cook for
25–30 minutes, until very tender. Stir in the butter
and serve with a drizzle of extra-virgin olive oil.
SERVES 6–8, TOGETHER WITH OTHER SIDE DISHES

Just because the winter cover has been put on the barbecue, it doesn't mean the fat lady's singing and the party's over. It's time to fire up the oven for Sunday lunch. There are three roasts and accompaniments on the following pages: mix and match as you will. For a winter party I like to serve two roasts with all three veggie plates.

SLOW ROASTED LAMB SHOULDER, ORANGE, ANCHOVY AND FENNEL

4 garlic cloves, chopped
6 rosemary sprigs, leaves from 3 finely chopped
4 anchovy fillets, chopped
zest and juice 1 orange
1 teaspoon fennel seeds
1 teaspoon dried chilli flakes
1 tablespoon olive oil
2kg lamb shoulder, bone in
2 fennel bulbs, sliced
1 onion, cut into wedges

Preheat the oven to 220°C/gas mark 7. Put the garlic, chopped rosemary, anchovy, orange zest, fennel seeds, chilli flakes and olive oil in a mortar and pestle with some salt and black pepper and grind to a rough paste. Use a sharp knife to make small incisions all over the lamb. Squeeze the juice of the orange over first, then rub the paste all over and into the meat.

Place the fennel and onion in the base of a large baking tray, sit the rosemary sprigs and lamb on top and roast for 20 minutes. Reduce the oven temperature to 150°C/gas mark 2 and roast for 4½ hours, checking every hour or so to ensure the tray doesn't dry out. Remove from the oven and allow to rest for 30 minutes before serving. SERVES 6

ROASTED CAULIFLOWER, SULTANAS AND PINE NUTS

1 large cauliflower, broken into florets,
  leaves reserved
2 tablespoons olive oil
75g pine nuts
65g sultanas
2 garlic cloves, sliced
1 pinch saffron strands
125ml chicken stock

Preheat the oven to 200°C/gas mark 6. Place the cauliflower florets in a roasting tin large enough to fit them in a singe layer. Drizzle over the olive oil and season with sea salt and freshly ground black pepper. Roast for 5 minutes.

Tear the cauliflower leaves into large pieces and add to the roasting tin with the pine nuts, sultanas and garlic. Roast for another 5 minutes, then add the saffron and stock. Stir the vegetables in the liquid and bake for a further 5 minutes, or until most of the liquid has been absorbed.

SERVES 6–8, TOGETHER WITH OTHER SIDE DISHES

ROASTED POTATOES AND PANCETTA

3 tablespoons olive oil
220g pancetta, chopped
1kg potatoes, peeled and cut into big chunks
6 garlic cloves, unpeeled and bashed
1 onion, cut into wedges
4 rosemary sprigs

Preheat the oven to 200°C/gas mark 6. Heat the oil in a large baking tray. Add the pancetta and fry on the stovetop over medium heat for 2 minutes, or until starting to release its oil and colour. Increase the heat, add the potatoes and stir to coat in the oils. Cook for 2–3 minutes on all sides. Scatter over the garlic, onion and rosemary with some sea salt and freshly ground black pepper. Transfer to the oven and cook for 1 hour, checking the potatoes and regularly giving the pan a shake.

SERVES 6–8, TOGETHER WITH OTHER SIDE DISHES

ROAST CHICKEN, SAFFRON, LEMON AND CHILLI

'Santo cielo!' I hear the gasps: 'What is the Australian madman up to now?' Actually, Italians tend towards magnanimous patience when the rest of us fiddle with their cuisine, so I'm hopeful they would taste this and smile: 'Yes, roast chicken with yoghurt. You have done well, Guglielmo.'

2 x 1.5kg free-range chickens
2 lemons, quartered
10 rosemary sprigs
2 red chillies, halved lengthways
2 garlic bulbs, halved through the centre
pinch saffron strands
150ml dry white wine
2 tablespoons olive oil
plain yoghurt, to serve

Preheat the oven to 180°C/gas mark 4. Generously season the cavity of the chickens with sea salt and freshly ground black pepper. Squeeze the lemon quarters over the skin then stuff them into the cavity with half the rosemary and a piece of chilli. Put the remaining rosemary in a baking tray with the chilli and halved garlic bulbs and sit the chickens on top.

Mix the saffron into the wine and pour over the chickens. Drizzle with olive oil, season with sea salt and roast for 1 hour, basting with the pan juices regularly. Allow to rest for 30 minutes before carving. Serve with any pan juices, a dollop of yoghurt on the side and your salad or vegetable of choice. **SERVES 8**

PORCHETTA AND ROASTED FRUIT

What a joy in life is porchetta. (I suspect I lost the vegetarian readership at 'mixed meat grill', so no point in holding back now.) If there are any leftovers, the pork is just as fabulous the next day, warmed up a little and served on a rosetta roll.

1 bunch sage, leaves picked and finely chopped
4 rosemary sprigs, leaves picked
   and finely chopped
4 thyme sprigs, leaves picked
   and finely chopped
3 garlic cloves, finely chopped,
   plus whole cloves, for roasting
2 tablespoons olive oil
2kg piece pork belly, skin on
2 teaspoons sea salt
2 onions, sliced
3 pears, halved
3 apples
1 orange, quartered

Put the sage, rosemary, thyme and chopped garlic in a mortar and pestle with half the olive oil and pound to a paste. Lay the pork skin side down and rub the paste all over the flesh. Roll up and secure with string. Set aside for 1 hour.

Preheat the oven to 220°C/gas mark 7. Rub the skin of the porchetta with the remaining oil and sprinkle with the sea salt. Place in a roasting tin and surround it with the garlic cloves, onions, pears, apples and orange. Roast for 30 minutes then toss the fruit and onions in the pan juices. Reduce the oven temperature to 160°C/gas mark 3 and roast for a further 2 hours. Remove from the oven, cover with foil and allow to rest for 30 minutes. Slice the pork and serve with the roasted fruit and onions. **SERVES 6**

My daughters decided that when we're in Italy we must eat a gelato a day. So, we step out at 5pm to take part in *la passeggiata*, ambling with the well-dressed Italian locals through the cooling streets while we decide where to eat dinner. This is when Italian children enjoy their sweet treat: a slice of cake or pastry from the *pasticceria*, or a chocolate gelato or sorbet. Italian after-dinner desserts are often more suited to the adult palate: the pastry is crumbly and nutty; the ices and jellies are tangy with bitter fruits; and the whole lot is often generously splashed with alcohol.

dolci
SWEETS

The Italians have perfected the technique of using alcohol to complement and contrast with the sweetness of fruit, cream and sugar. Vin Santo, used here, is a Tuscan dessert wine, but any sweet wine will work the same magic.

ROASTED SEASONAL FRUIT, ALMONDS AND MASCARPONE CREAM

1kg seasonal fruit (I used pears,
    peaches and plums)
45g butter, softened
3 tablespoons demerara sugar
seeds from 1 vanilla pod
1 teaspoon ground cinnamon
125ml Vin Santo
60g blanched almonds, roughly chopped
for the mascarpone cream
200g mascarpone cheese
125ml double cream
1 tablespoon Vin Santo

To make the mascarpone cream, beat the mascarpone with electric beaters for a few minutes until soft, then beat in the cream and the Vin Santo until soft peaks form.

Preheat the oven to 200°C/gas mark 6. Cut the fruit into wedges, removing the stones and the cores, and place in a baking tray. Mix the butter, sugar, vanilla seeds and cinnamon together and dot over the fruit. Pour in the wine and bake for 30 minutes, or until the fruit is starting to soften. Scatter the almonds over the fruit, return the tray to the oven and bake for a further 10 minutes, or until the nuts are golden. Serve with the mascarpone cream and any pan syrup spooned over the top.
SERVES 4

YOGHURT PANNACOTTA, CHERRIES AND HONEYCOMB

200ml double cream
180ml milk
80g caster sugar
4 leaves gelatine
200g Greek yoghurt, at room temperature
fresh honeycomb, to serve
for the poached cherries
345g cherries, pitted
3 tablespoons caster sugar
½ teaspoon vanilla extract
1 tablespoon Marsala

Gently heat the cream, milk and sugar in a small saucepan, stirring to dissolve the sugar. Bring to a simmer and immediately remove from the heat. Soak the gelatine in cold water until soft. Squeeze out the excess water, drop the gelatine into the hot cream mixture and whisk until dissolved. In a bowl, add the mixture to the yoghurt, whisking as you go, until smooth. Pour into four 150ml moulds or small glasses. Cover with cling film and chill for at least 6 hours, or overnight.

To poach the cherries, put the cherries in a saucepan with the sugar, vanilla extract, Marsala and 3 tablespoons water. Place over low heat and stir until the sugar has dissolved, then increase the heat to a simmer and cook for 1 minute. Set aside to cool.

To serve, dip the moulds into hot water for a few seconds, invert onto plates and lift off the moulds. Serve with the cherries and a piece of honeycomb.
SERVES 4

PISTACHIO AND ORANGE LOAF CAKE

220g unsalted butter, softened
220g caster sugar
3 eggs, lightly beaten
grated zest and juice 1 orange
200g plain flour
125g pistachios (shelled weight),
   very finely ground
2 teaspoons baking powder
2 tablespoons honey

Preheat the oven to 180°C/gas mark 4. Lightly grease a 900g/2lb loaf tin and line with baking paper. Beat the butter and sugar with electric beaters until the mixture is thick and pale. Add the egg, a little at a time, beating continually, then stir in the orange zest and juice.

Mix together the flour, pistachios and baking powder and fold into the cake batter. Spoon into the prepared tin and bake for 40–50 minutes, or until a skewer inserted into the centre comes out dry. Cover the cake loosely with foil while baking if the top starts to get too much colour.

Remove the cake from the oven. Heat the honey in a saucepan until runny and brush over the top of the cake. Cool on a cake rack before turning out.
SERVES 8

CHOCOLATE AND HAZELNUT CAKE WITH NUTELLA FROSTING

185g dark chocolate (70% cocoa solids),
   coarsely chopped
5 eggs, separated
220g caster sugar
300g toasted hazelnuts, very finely ground
for the topping
180g Nutella
220g mascarpone cheese
150g toasted hazelnuts

Preheat the oven to 160°C/gas mark 3. Lightly grease a 25cm springform cake tin and line with baking paper. Melt the chocolate in a bowl over a pan of simmering water. Set aside to cool. Beat the egg yolks and half the sugar until pale and frothy. Fold in the melted chocolate and ground hazelnuts.

In a clean metal bowl, whisk the egg whites with a pinch of salt until stiff. Gradually add the remaining sugar until very firm and glossy. Stir a quarter of the whisked egg white into the chocolate mixture to loosen it, then gently fold in the remainder. Tip into the prepared tin and bake for 1 hour, covering the cake loosely with foil if the top starts to get too much colour. Cool on a cake rack before turning out onto a plate.

For the topping, whisk together the Nutella and mascarpone until well combined. Spread over the cake, scatter with the hazelnuts and serve. **SERVES 8-10**

To say the children were keen to try this 'nutella' cake is an understatement. (It could unfairly be compared to watching truffle pigs pick up the scent.) Of all the recipes I've ever written, for any book, this is the one they've loved the most. And, before I discover myself pilloried for poor food choices, let me quickly add: enjoy in moderation; just a tiny sliver, every two years or so!

BAKED RICOTTA CHEESECAKE

125g amaretti biscuits
125g digestive biscuits
125g butter, melted and cooled
400g strawberries, hulled and halved, to serve
for the filling
4 eggs
115g caster sugar
600g ricotta cheese
150g mascarpone cheese
50g plain flour
grated zest 1 lemon, plus squeeze juice

Preheat the oven to 180°C/gas mark 4. Lightly grease a 23cm springform cake tin and line with baking paper. Put the amaretti and digestive biscuits in a large sealable bag and crush with a rolling pin until fine crumbs. Tip into a bowl, add the butter and mix until all the crumbs are coated. Transfer the crumbs to the prepared tin and spread evenly over the base. Bake for 10 minutes. Remove from the oven and allow to cool. Reduce the oven temperature to 160°C/gas mark 3.

To make the filling, lightly beat the eggs and sugar until the sugar has dissolved. Add the ricotta, mascarpone, flour and lemon zest and squeeze of juice and continue beating until well combined.

Pour the filling over the biscuit base. Bake for 45 minutes, or until just set with a slight wobble in the middle. Switch off the oven, open the door a little and leave the cheesecake to cool completely. Spoon strawberries over the top before serving.

SERVES 8–10

ORANGE AND CAMPARI GRANITA

750ml freshly squeezed orange juice
180ml Campari, plus extra to serve
juice 1 lemon
4 tablespoons caster sugar

Stir all the ingredients together in a jug until the sugar has dissolved. Pour into a shallow freezer tray and freeze for about 1 hour, until the mixture is solid around the edge and slushy in the middle. Use a fork to stir the outside crystals into the centre. Return to the freezer and freeze for 30 minutes. Remove and repeat the stirring process every half hour or so, until you have evenly sized crystals throughout. Spoon into glasses and serve with an extra shot of Campari if you like. **SERVES 4**

PROSECCO AND POMEGRANATE JELLY

5 leaves gelatine
75cl bottle Prosecco
60g caster sugar
seeds from 1 pomegranate
4 tablespoons gin

Soak the gelatine in cold water. Heat 4 tablespoons Prosecco, 3 tablespoons water and the sugar in a saucepan over a low heat, stirring until the sugar has dissolved. Remove from the heat.

Remove the gelatine from the water and squeeze out any excess. Add to the pan and stir until fully dissolved. Allow to cool slightly. Transfer to a jug with the remaining Prosecco and stir. Pour into a plastic container and chill for at least 4 hours, or until set. While you wait, lay the pomegranate seeds in a single layer on a tray and freeze until solid.

To serve, layer up scoops of jelly and frozen pomegranate seeds in four small glasses, pour 1 tablespoon of gin over each and mix lightly. **SERVES 4**

These beautiful icy desserts typify the Italian way to end a meal:
clean tangy flavours, laced (liberally) with alcohol and definitely
not for the bambini. Serve these in shot glasses for a party.

If making a tart for a super-quick dessert sounds a crazy idea, think again. This is the simplest of dishes, using a rough butter pastry pressed into the tin. If you've already made the plum and vanilla compote (page 50), just spoon it in and dollop with yoghurt.

PLUM, VANILLA AND ALMOND TART

for the base
140g butter, melted and cooled,
    plus extra for greasing
115g caster sugar
200g plain flour, plus extra for dusting
4 tablespoons ground almonds
for the filling
plum and vanilla compote (see page 50)
60g roasted almonds, roughly chopped
260g Greek yoghurt

Preheat the oven to 180°C/gas mark 4 and grease and line a square 20cm tart tin. Mix the butter and sugar together then stir in the flour and almonds. Patch the pastry over the base and up the sides, pressing with your fingers to get an even case. Chill for 15 minutes.

Scrunch up a piece of baking paper and use it to line the pastry case. Add baking beans and bake for 15 minutes. Remove from the oven, tip out the baking beans and paper and return to the oven for a further 5–10 minutes, or until the pastry is golden and crisp. Allow to cool.

To serve, spoon the compote into the tart case, scatter with the almonds and dollops of yoghurt.
SERVES 6

MIXED BERRIES, ZABAGLIONE AND AMARETTI

500g mixed berries, such as raspberries,
    blackberries, strawberries and redcurrants
juice ½ lemon
2 teaspoons caster sugar
6 amaretti biscuits
<u>for the zabaglione</u>
3 egg yolks
3 tablespoons caster sugar
60ml Marsala

Place the berries in a bowl, halving any large
strawberries. Gently stir in the lemon juice and
sugar and set aside.

To make the zabaglione, use electric beaters to
whisk together the egg yolks, sugar and Marsala in
a heatproof bowl, until frothy. Rest the bowl over
a pan of simmering water and continue whisking for
5–6 minutes, until the mixture is light, frothy and
almost trebled in volume. Remove from the heat.

Divide the berries between four plates and spoon
over the zabaglione. Crumble the amaretti biscuits
over the top and serve. SERVES 4

This is my idea of dessert perfection: great taste with no work required. (And surely the only way to improve on perfection is by adding dark chocolate?) Affogato was perhaps discovered when a waiter slipped and 'drowned' a diner's ice-cream in coffee. Or, by a lazy genius who invited friends for dinner but had nothing in the kitchen except ice-cream and a cup of coffee?

CHOCOLATE AFFOGATO

4 scoops good-quality vanilla ice-cream
4 shots espresso
60g dark chocolate, roughly chopped

Put a scoop of ice-cream into four small coffee cups or glasses, pour a shot of freshly brewed espresso over each one and scatter with the chocolate before serving. **SERVES 4**

VANILLA ICE-CREAM AND VIN SANTO RAISINS

125ml Vin Santo
90g raisins
500g tub vanilla ice-cream
75g toasted pistachios, chopped

Heat the wine to boiling point. Remove from the heat, add the raisins and set aside for 1 hour.

Serve vanilla ice-cream with the soaked raisins spooned over and topped with pistachios. **SERVES 4**

INDEX

FOR NATALIE, EDIE, INÈS AND BUNNY This book was conceived during a baking-hot family summer holiday in Puglia, the 'heel' of the 'boot' that is Italy. Its somewhat brutal landscape, warm welcoming people and honest earthy rustic food inspired a cooking bonanza and a collection of 'my version of' Italian recipes. My family devoured the spoils, even when they included a novice's attempt at wood-fired pizza. I am so grateful for the opportunity to create this book and thank HarperCollins for their continuing trust and faith in my work. I am enormously thankful to the team of hard-working individuals who made this book a reality: Lou, for her inspired design and art direction and for keeping us organised against all odds; my food team, Julian, Rosie, Marina and Kathy, who ensured the food looked as delicious as it tastes (Julian, you do create a beautiful mess, and Marina, you work wonders); Erika and Mikkel, whose passion and bounce are contagious and awe-inspiring, at sun-up and sun-down; Lucy, for trawling the flea markets for such gems of props, and Tamin, for your patience and calm, no matter where you found yourself; to my wordsmiths, Glenda, for uncompromising attention to detail, and Jane, for often knowing what I mean better than I do myself; Paul and Pete, the images sing due to your expertise; Victoria, you keep us all on our toes; and Antony, your knowledge guides us to higher levels. On our shoot we found ourselves back in the stunning house, Secondo Amore, thanks to the patient kind Katy Lake from Think Puglia who encouraged the owners to allow our team to mine its beauty. We grew into an extended family with our adopted Italians, Anna Maria and her son, Pasquale. Anna Maria taught the girls to make orecchiette and showered us with Pugliese hospitality on our first visit; this time they both went to the ends of the earth to help us all. Guiding us through the language and the local terrain was the immaculately dressed Mario. (Please can we borrow your grandmother's meat slicer?) And none of it would have been possible without the local community of Ostuni – fishmonger, baker and grocer – who, no doubt, could not fathom what we wanted with so much food every day!

Creative Director Erika Oliveira
Photograper Mikkel Vang
Art Director Louise Davids
Editor Glenda Downing
Contributing Editor Jane Price
Food Editor Marina Filippelli
Food Stylists Julian Biggs, Rosie Reynolds
Recipe Testing Kathy Kordalis
Prop Stylist Lucy Attwater
Local Assistant Mario De Palma
Photography Assistant Tamin Jones
Contributing Designers Mary Libro, Annette Fitzgerald
Script Illustrator Gavin Kirk
Production Manager Victoria Jefferys
Prepress Paul Aikman, Graphic Print Group
Producer Natalie Elliott

All spoon measures are level unless otherwise stated and 1 tablespoon equals 20ml.

Cooking temperatures and times relate to conventional ovens. If you are using a fan-assisted oven, set the oven temperature 20 degrees lower. For baking, I recommend a conventional oven rather than a fan-assisted oven.

Anyone who is pregnant or in a vulnerable health group should consult their doctor regarding eating raw or lightly cooked eggs.

First published in 2014 by HarperCollins *Publishers*

77-85 Fulham Palace Road
Hammersmith
London, W6 8JB
www.harpercollins.co.uk

10 9 8 7 6 5 4 3 2 1

Text © 2014 William Granger
Photography © 2014 Mikkel Vang
Design and layout © 2014 bills Licensing Pty Limited

A catalogue record of this book is available from the British Library

ISBN: 978-0-00-750700-9

Printed and bound by South China Printing Company Ltd

www.bill-granger.com